pillsbury publications

Pillsbury's Meat Cook Book

Meat recipes and menu ideas
for all occasions

Dear Homemaker,

Meat is generally recognized as the star attraction in most meals. Pillsbury Publications is happy to bring you a cook book of meat recipes and menu ideas to make mealtime a pleasure for both family and guests.

In using this book you'll find ideas when you're looking for something new for dinner, or you've already bought a cut of meat and you're wondering how to make it a little special, or you're looking for a recipe that is a family favorite. To assure you of high quality and dependable results, our Publications home economists have developed and tested the recipes with the different conditions you might find in your own kitchen.

Additional information includes recipes for meat salads and soups, sauces and gravies, outdoor cooking, leftovers, hints on economizing and make-ahead dishes, cooking with wine and meat carving illustrations.

To make meat selection easier, we have provided basic information on meat inspection, gradation, purchase and storage. Color photographs identify the wide variety of meat cuts you see in your supermarket. We would like to thank the National Live Stock and Meat Board for their kind assistance and expert advice.

We hope this cook book will serve you as both a daily resource in your meal planning and also as a stimulus to your own creativity.

Cordially,

Dianne Hennesy King

Dianne Hennesy King
Editor, Pillsbury Publications

Contents

Meat is usually the focal point of meals and meal planning — especially for dinner. As one of the most popular foods, it serves an important role in supplying the essential nutrients and interest variety for you and your family.

A very wide range of various meat cuts can be found in most grocery stores today. This book explains these cuts and gives recipes for preparing them. A new cut of meat or a familiar one that's fixed in a new way can help you add new interest to meals — whether they are family or company, budget or special occasion.

Purchasing and storing meat wisely helps you make the most of the meat you buy. We've given some hints to make these steps easier for you and have also included tips for cooking meat from the frozen state, cooking with wine, planning meals, economizing with meat, using leftovers and cooking for small families.

The meat recipes have been grouped according to the kind and cut of meat which they use. Since barbecue favorites, meaty main dish salads, gravies and sauces can use several types of meat, the recipes for these have

been placed in special chapters toward the end of the book.

Each recipe is accompanied by a suggestion for serving that dish. Use these suggestions as idea stimulators for incorporating your own family's favorites into your meals. In the tips that follow the recipes, you'll find information on ingredient substitutions, method variations, make-ahead and freezing guidelines, and suggestions for halving recipes for smaller families. Roasting charts and carving instructions are included by the recipes for many of the large cuts of meat, and recipes using leftovers follow the recipes for roasts.

The last chapter contains basic information on the nutritional value of meat and its contribution to overall daily eating patterns.

The flour in these recipes does not need to be sifted. All of the recipes in this book have been tested by simply spooning the flour lightly into the cup and leveling with a spatula or knife. Both Pillsbury All Purpose and Pillsbury Self-Rising Flours have been used in developing the recipes in this book. Self-rising flour includes added leavenings and salt, so refer to the Tips for instructions for its substitution.

We've found that no high altitude (5,200 feet) adjustments are necessary for the recipes we've included. However, when a time range is given for simmering meats with liquid, it may be necessary to regularly use the longer time in order to insure tenderness of the meat.

All of these helps are designed to make the recipes convenient for you to use and to give you freedom in tailoring these recipes to your own family's preferences. Have a good time planning and preparing your meals and your family is bound to enjoy them. You'll enjoy the boost that an attractively served meal can give your creative ego. The ideas in this book can be an inspiration for your imagination. Bon Appétit

Braised Pork Chops, Page 61

4

Basic information

The government requires that all fresh meat which is transported across state lines to be sold commercially be inspected federally. The purpose of this inspection is to guarantee every consumer that the fresh meat which is purchased is wholesome and has been processed under strict sanitary conditions. An inspection stamp appears on all meat products which pass the federal inspection. The purple fluid used for this stamp is made from a harmless vegetable coloring and does not need to be trimmed from the meat before preparing. (The number which appears on the stamp stands for the place at which the meat was inspected.)

Processed meats also bear a federal stamp of inspection which signifies that they are made from wholesome meat, have been processed under strict sanitary conditions, and have been truthfully labeled. Meat which is not inspected federally can be inspected by a similar state inspection system.

In addition to being inspected, meat and meat products are also graded according to overall quality and tenderness. The top grade of meat, U.S.D.A. PRIME, is most frequently used by restaurants and hotels, although some supermarkets and specialty stores do carry it. Most meat which is found in supermarkets is graded U.S.D.A. CHOICE or U.S.D.A. GOOD. The two lower grades, U.S.D.A. STANDARD and U.S.D.A. COMMERCIAL, are rarely sold on the retail market.

Since the grading of meat is voluntary, some packers and retailers use their own brand names to signify the various grades of their meat and meat products. The grade assigned to meat is generally a clue to the tenderness and quality of the meat that you can expect, if you prepare it properly. The most tender steak can be tough and uninviting if it is cooked incorrectly. And likewise, a less tender cut of meat can be delicious if it is prepared to its best advantage.

All grades of meat, though, contain the same valuable nutrients — protein, minerals, and vitamins — which the body needs.

Storing meat properly is essential in order to assure you that the meat you've selected will still be of high quality when you prepare it. Fresh, cured and ready-to-eat meats are all perishable. To preserve their nutritive value and high quality, they should be refrigerated or frozen as soon as possible after purchasing. Warm or room temperatures foster the growth of the microorganisms and also speed spoilage.

MEAT BUYING AND STORING TIPS

Meat selection is often one of the most difficult tasks. The variety of names used for a particular cut plus the continuing change going on with meat names can be very discouraging. By learning a few basics about the distinctive appearance of particular meat cuts, you need not be confused when it appears with a new name. If you aren't sure about a cut, ask where it comes from in relation to cuts you are familiar with — it makes a big difference if it comes from the T-bone steak area or if it comes from the pot-roast area. You must know what you're buying in order to cook it so that it will be tender and flavorful.

Some thoughts to keep in mind when selecting meat:

1. Meat becomes less tender with age. For example, most cuts of veal and lamb (young animals) are tender, but only certain portions of beef are tender.

2. Meat becomes less tender with exercise. For example, a beef chuck (shoulder), where pot-roasts come from, has much more exercise than the back where tender steaks come from.

3. Although exercise makes meat less tender, it does develop flavor. For example, some people prefer the delicate flavor of tenderloin steak (receives almost no exercise) whereas, some prefer the heartier flavor of a sirloin steak (receives moderate exercise). A tender steak would make poor stew meat because the juices would have little flavor.

4. The shoulder (chuck) and round areas are often confused since both may have a round bone (arm in shoulder, leg in round). In all meats — beef, veal, pork and lamb — the shoulder consists of many muscles running in various directions. In addition, many shoulder cuts also include a portion of the blade bone. Meats from this area usually cost less per pound because there are more cuts from this section than from the tender loin section. Also there's some-

times more waste. Meats from the round area have about 3 large solid muscles all running in the same direction. Since there is less exercise here, the cuts tend to be slightly more tender.

5. Any cut of meat can be made tender with proper cooking. Tender, delicate flavored cuts (like T-bone steak) are best cooked quickly without added water. A less tender cut is best cooked with liquid; the long cooking with liquid tenderizes the less tender meat tissues. Some tenderizing of less tender meats can result from marinating in a marinade for several hours or overnight. Most marinades contain lemon juice, vinegar or wine — the acid in these helps soften and tenderize the less tender tissues.

STORAGE OF MEAT:

- Store in the coldest part of refrigerator without actually freezing the meat. A refrigerator meat storage compartment is especially designed for optimum temperature and humidity.

- Pre-packaged meats can be stored in the refrigerator in their original wrappings for 1 to 2 days. For longer storage (up to 3 days) unwrap meat and cover loosely — some air helps retard bacteria growth. Large cuts of meat (roasts) can be stored 5 to 6 days. Ground meats should be used within 24 hours. If you find you cannot use the meat right away, freeze it and cook later; or cook, freeze and reheat later to serve.

- Fresh meat which has not been pre-packaged should be loosely rewrapped before refrigeration.

- You can freeze meat in original packaging for short storage, 1 to 2 weeks. For longer storage, overwrap or rewrap the meat in moisture-vapor proof material and store in freezer at 0° or lower. Freezing is not recommended for canned hams and other canned meats since freezing sometimes causes seams in the can to break.

- Meat which has not been tightly wrapped before freezing may appear whitish and dry. This is called ''freezer burn''. It is a result of being exposed to the air and dehydrating. It is not harmful, but the meat may be somewhat tough and tasteless after it has been cooked.

- Place meats to be frozen close to the wall of your freezer until they are frozen. The faster meat is frozen, the more of its quality will be retained.

- Leftover meats which have been cooked should be cooled as quickly as possible and stored, covered, in the refrigerator. Leave meat in as large pieces as possible, so that the least amount of moisture will be lost from the meat during storage.

- To make defrosting easier, package meats to be frozen in ready-to-use sizes and label according to the type of meat, amount, and date of purchase.

- Refreezing meat which has been defrosted is not recommended except in emergencies. Some loss of juices occurs during defrosting, and the meat is apt to be less juicy if it has been defrosted twice before cooking.

- Meat should be left wrapped when defrosting, either in the refrigerator or at room temperature. If you defrost the meat at room temperature, it should be refrigerated immediately after it has completely thawed.

- Ground or mechanically tenderized meat is more susceptible to spoilage because of the greater surface area that's exposed to air and bacteria.

COOKING FROM THE FROZEN STATE

Most recipes for cooking meat assume either that the meat has not been frozen or that it has been defrosted before cooking begins. It is possible, however, to cook meat from the frozen state — if additional time is allowed for the thawing that must occur during cooking. Frozen roasts must cook about ⅓ to ½ longer than unfrozen roasts of the same size. Cook frozen roasts at 300° to 325°. A meat thermometer (inserted after thawing during cooking) is your best indicator for doneness (see page 9).

Additional time required to cook frozen steaks, chops or patties depends on the thickness, as well as the amount of surface area.

To broil, place frozen meat further from the heat.

To cook in a fry pan, cook quickly over high heat until browned on both sides (otherwise, moisture from defrosting will slow down the browning). Reduce heat after meat has browned and then cook slowly, allowing meat to cook thoroughly.

Meats that are to be breaded or floured must be at least partially thawed so that the mixture will stick to the surface.

Meats which will be cooked in liquid need less additional cooking time because the meats will thaw more quickly in hot water.

Freezing casserole dishes is not always time-saving. Some foods take less time to prepare fresh than frozen. However, a freezer stocked with two or three ready-prepared casseroles can be a life saver for unexpected guests or quick, busy-day meals. Casserole dishes and stews freeze best if they are made with enough sauce so that the solid pieces are completely covered during freezing. Do not over-cook them when preparing for freezing. Cool thoroughly, cover and seal with foil before freezing. Thaw in the refrigerator or at room tempera-ture. If thawing at room temperature, refrigerate once thawed if it is not to be heated immediately.

Timetable for Thawing Meat:

	At Room Temp. Hrs. per lb.	In Refrigerator Hrs. per lb.
Large roast	2 to 3 hrs.	4 to 7 hrs.
Small roast	1 to 2 hrs.	3 to 5 hrs.
1-inch steak	2 to 4 hrs.	12 to 14 hrs.

How to Judge When Meat is Spoiled:

Meat that is spoiling changes from a bright red for beef and lamb (pink for pork and veal) to a dull greyed color. The surface may become slippery, and the meat develops a pronounced off-odor. When an off-odor has developed, the meat should be discarded.

STORAGE TIME CHART

Maximum storage time recommendations for Fresh, Cooked and Processed Meat

MEAT	FREEZER (at 0° F. or lower)*	REFRIGERATOR (38° to 40° F.)
Beef (fresh)	6 to 12 months	2 to 4 days
Veal (fresh)	6 to 9 months	2 to 4 days
Pork (fresh)	3 to 6 months	2 to 4 days
Lamb (fresh)	6 to 9 months	2 to 4 days
Ground beef, veal and lamb	3 to 4 months	1 to 2 days
Ground pork	1 to 3 months	1 to 2 days
Variety meats	3 to 4 months	1 to 2 days
Luncheon meats	not recommended	1 week
Sausage, fresh pork	60 days	1 week
Sausage, smoked	2 to 3 weeks	3 to 7 days
Sausage, dry and semi-dry (unsliced)	not recommended	2 to 3 weeks
Wieners	3 to 4 weeks	4 to 5 days
Bacon	3 to 4 weeks	5 to 7 days
Smoked ham, whole	60 days	1 week
Ham slices	2 to 3 weeks	3 to 4 days
Beef, corned	2 weeks	1 week
Leftover cooked meat	2 to 3 months	4 to 5 days
Frozen Combination Foods		
Meat pies (cooked)	3 months	
Swiss steak (cooked)	3 months	
Stews (cooked)	3 to 4 months	
Prepared meat dinners	2 to 6 months	

*Some refrigerator freezers do not reach 0° F. Meat can still be frozen at temperatures above 0° F. but should not be kept for the maximum time. Consult your operator's manual for information on the freezing temperature of your freezer.

Cranberry Stuffed Pork Crown Roast, page 58

8

MEAT THERMOMETERS

Meat thermometers register the internal temperature (degree of doneness) of the meat. They should be inserted into the center of the thickest portion of meat, being sure that the bulb of the thermometer doesn't rest in fat or on bone. See specific recipes for the approximate roasting times.

Beef: Doneness of meat can be gauged as follows:
140° rare
160° medium
170° well

Veal: Since veal is always cooked well-done, doneness is indicated by a reading of 170°.

Fresh Pork: Since pork is always cooked well-done, the doneness of pork is indicated by a reading of 170°.

Cured and Smoked Pork: "Cook-before-eating" hams need to be cooked well-done, indicated by 160°. "Fully-cooked" cuts are ready to eat when the thermometer reaches 130°.

Lamb: Since lamb is usually cooked well-done, the doneness of lamb is indicated by a reading of 165 to 170°.

To use an automatic meat probe in roasting meats, insert probe into the thickest part of the muscle, making sure the probe doesn't rest in fat or on bone. Automatic meat probes can also be used in broiling cuts of meat that are at least 1½-inches thick.

Meat carving can be made easy if a few simple rules are observed. The meat should be properly cooked and large roasts allowed to stand 15 to 20 minutes before carving.

Remove strings and skewers before carving unless they are essential for holding the meat together.

Hold the meat firmly in place and slice meat across the grain (except for steaks and ham slices). By slicing meat across the grain, the meat fibers are

shortened and the slices seem more tender. Meats (such as Flank Steak and Corned Beef Brisket) that are too thin to slice across the grain can be sliced diagonally.

A variety of cutlery sets are available. Use the set with which you feel most comfortable.

Standard carving set: The knife usually has 8 or 9-inch curved blade. The tines of the fork are spaced closely together and have a guard. A steel to sharpen the edge of the knife before carving is usually included in this set. This is an excellent set for general use and is especially good for medium-sized pieces of meat.

Steak carving set: The knife has a 6 or 7-inch blade which is slightly curved. The tines of the fork are closely spaced. This set is ideal for steaks, chops and large ham slices.

Roast meat slicer and carver's helper: The knife blade is narrow and straight-edged, about 11 inches long. The tines of the fork are widely spaced to hold the roast firmly.

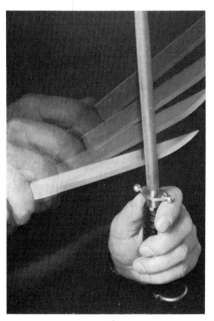

To sharpen a knife, hold sharpening steel firmly in left hand (with thumb on top of handle). Place the end of the blade near the handle against the far side of the sharpening steel.

Bring blade down along the steel in a sweeping motion, so that the entire length of the blade passes lightly over the steel.

Bring knife back into the starting position with the blade on the near side of the sharpening steel this time. Repeat stroking motion. Continue alternating strokes until edge is sharpened.

Electric knife sharpeners and roll-type knife sharpeners are also available — and handy to use.

Minute Steak Lorraine, page 37

Cooking with Wines

Cooking with wine is an old tradition that began centuries ago when Europeans found that the ordinary, less expensive cuts of meat and fish could be transformed into exciting dishes by adding wine during cooking. It's amazing what wine can do to help you make dishes more provocative and interesting without spending a lot of money.

Only very small quantities of wine are used in cooking. Since the alcohol evaporates during the cooking process, the only reason to use wine is for flavor. A good sound rule is to cook with the wine you drink — and vice versa. Small amounts of leftover dinner wines are great for using in cooking, and every wine type known can be used. However, wines that are specifically labeled ''Cooking Wines'' have had a small amount of salt added to them.

Cooking with wine is not complicated. Wine can be added without a recipe — just like salt, pepper or any other condiment — according to your taste. You can develop some of your own specialties by trying different wines in cooking a variety of foods. Even prepared mixes and other convenience foods take on individuality when you cook them with wine.

Some of the recipes we've included in this book call for wine or give its use as an option. If you enjoy cooking with wine, you may want to try adding wine to some of the other recipes in this book, too.

As a general rule, use the wine that is the natural partner for the food you are preparing. When you don't have a recipe to guide you, the following chart can serve as a guide for basic proportions and type of wine to use. Substitute the amount of wine for part of the liquid in whatever recipe you choose to use.

WINE COOKERY CHART

FOODS	AMOUNT OF WINE Per Cup Liquid	WINES
SOUPS		
Cream soups	1 T. per cup	Sauterne or sherry
Meat and vegetable soups	1 T. per cup	Red wine or sherry
SAUCES		
Cream sauce & variations	1 T. per cup	Sherry or white wine
Brown sauce & variations	1 T. per cup	Sherry or red wine
Tomato sauces	1 T. per cup	Sherry or red wine
Cheese sauces	1 T. per cup	Sherry or white wine
MEATS AND GAME		
Pot-roast and other beef cuts	¼ cup per lb.	Red wines
Gravy for roasts	2 T. per cup	Red or white wines
Stew — beef	¼ cup per lb.	Red wines
Stew — lamb and veal	¼ cup per lb.	Red wines
Ham, baked	2 cups (for basting)	Port or muscatel
Liver, braised	¼ cup per lb.	Red or white wines
Tongue, boiled	½ cup per lb.	Red wines

SUBSTITUTIONS

Bouillon . . . 1 cube bouillon = 1 teaspoon instant bouillon

Chives . . . 1 tablespoon freeze-dried or frozen = 1 tablespoon chopped fresh

Garlic . . . ⅛ teaspoon garlic powder or ½ teaspoon garlic salt = 1 medium clove garlic

Herbs . . . ¼ teaspoon ground herbs = 1 teaspoon leaf herbs

Onion . . . 1 tablespoon instant minced = ⅓ cup chopped fresh

1 tablespoon dried onion flakes = ¼ cup chopped fresh

1 tablespoon onion salt = ¼ cup chopped fresh

Parsley . . . 1 tablespoon dried parsley flakes = 3 tablespoons chopped fresh parsley

Sweet pepper . . . 1 tablespoon sweet pepper flakes = 2 tablespoons chopped fresh green and red peppers

ECONOMIZING

The greatest portion of most food budgets is spent on meat products. So, naturally you want to be sure you get the most for your money.

The price per pound is not always the best clue to the bargain value of a meat cut. Because various cuts of meat contain different amounts of fat and bone, the amount of lean tissue (the part you eat) is also bound to vary. Since the number of servings that can be obtained from one pound will depend upon the amount of bone and fat waste, the best way to figure the bargain value of your meat is on the basis of the cost per serving.

Guide for Amount of Meat to Purchase:

You may use the following as a general guide. Take into consideration, too, your family's eating habits and the other foods that will be served with the meal.

Meat with no bone and very little fat — ¼ to ⅓ lb. per serving.

Meat with small amount of bone and little fat — ⅓ to ½ lb. per serving.

Meat with large amount of bone and little fat — ¾ to 1 lb. per serving.

Buy meat that has been well-trimmed of excess fat. A chop with a minimal amount of attached fat would be a better buy per pound than one with liberal amounts of fat. When you buy by the pound, extra fat that you won't eat is not a bargain.

If a cut of lean, boneless meat (such as Rolled Rump Roast) were featured at 99¢ per lb., one serving would cost approximately 25¢ because there would be no waste from bone or excess fat. (One lb. gives 4 servings; 99¢ divided by 4 = 25¢.)

A cut of the same meat with some bone (Rump Roast) featured at 89¢ per lb. would cost approximately 30¢ per serving. (One lb. gives only 3 servings; 89¢ divided by 3 = 30¢.)

Two factors which influence the prices at which stores sell various meat cuts are the popularity of the cut and its availability. Also, less tender cuts of meat are most often priced at savings. These can be prepared flavorfully and tenderized by cooking them with liquid. We hope you become acquainted with some of our recipes for these cuts of meats.

Periodic specials that are featured by your grocery store at a lower price per pound can aid you in spending your food dollar wisely. Check your newspaper for advertised bargains.

Grocery stores frequently feature meat specials, including roasts, pot-roasts, steaks, chops and ground meat. Large families can easily take advantage of both the large and small cuts when specials such as these are offered. For smaller families the larger cuts are usually more meat — even though at a good price — than they can consume in one meal. This sometimes can mean several left-over meals that look very much alike.

With a little bit of advance planning, though, and some cutting, you can divide these large, economical cuts of meat into several different-looking and different-tasting meals. Freeze or refrigerate some of the cuts for later use, rather than cooking the whole cut all at one time.

When bones are involved, you will need the assistance of your meat man. Otherwise, a sharp knife is all you need to divide these economical cuts into easy-to-use portions for your family. Refer to the pages given in parenthesis for recipes using each particular cut. These are only a few of the many recipes in which they could be used. Most any recipe in which the same cut of meat is specified can be used to prepare the following cuts.

A whole Pork Boston Shoulder Roast usually weighs about 5 to 7 lbs. and has a small amount of bone. This cut can easily be divided at home into portions for three freshly cooked meals — a roast (page 58), boneless steaks (page 61), and cubed pork (page 66) for a casserole dish. Divide the large roast into two pieces by cutting across the roast with a very sharp knife. The section with the bone can be used for the pork roast. From the remaining section, pork steaks can be cut. (Cook them like you would pork chops.) The small end of the boneless piece can be cut into cubes and used in a meat-stretching dish.

Hams are available in two halves — the butt half (closer to the body) and the shank half (including the leg joint). You can conveniently take advantage of a full shank half by dividing a 6 to 8 lb. ham into sections for three freshly cooked meals. Ask your meat man to cut off a generous shank end; this makes the basis for a great boiled dinner, soup, etc. (page 68). You can easily divide the remaining center part by cutting it into two portions. The section with the bone can be baked (page 73); the remainder can be cut into boneless ham slices, cubes, or very thin slices — as you wish.

Large Pork Loin Roasts can be conveniently sectioned with the assistance of your meat man. Have him slice between the ribs on one end, making chops (page 61), but leaving about 3 to 4 lbs. for your Pork Roast (page 58).

Larger Legs of Lamb (7 to 9 lbs.) can be divided several ways for convenient eating. Because the cutting involves a sizeable bone, you will need to plan this one in advance and ask your meat man to do the cutting for you. Cut slices from the sirloin end of the leg; these lamb steaks can be prepared as you would prepare loin chops (page 94). At the other end, ask your meat man to cut off the shank portion. This can be used whole (page 98) or can be cut into boneless cubes for stews, etc. (page 97). The remaining center portion of the leg makes a delicious lamb roast (page 91).

Arm cuts and round bone pot-roasts are cut differently in various sections of the country. However, if you do find a large round bone pot-roast, it too can be sectioned for several freshly cooked meals. Cut off a section from the round end of the roast; cube it and use it as you would stew meat (page 49). The remaining piece with the bone makes as good a pot-roast (page 23) as the original whole roast.

Learn the value of variety meats for nutrition, as well as economy. Since most of the different types of variety meats can be substituted for each other (veal for beef, etc.) watch for individual bargains.

If freezer space is available, it may be to your advantage to stock up when such sales come along. However, if you have no place to store extra meat and cannot eat it within the desired time range, spoiled meat can't be a bargain to you — regardless of the price.

Illustrations courtesy of the American Meat Institute.

MEAL PLANNING

The real success of any meal is in the planning, as well as in the cooking. Attractive combinations of food appeal to the eyes just as delicious aromas stimulate the appetite. You can probably judge which foods appeal to your family and which accompanying dishes they like with these. You can utilize this information to its fullest and express your creative ability by planning meals with a consideration to aesthetic appeal. Mix and vary the colors, shapes, flavors, textures and temperatures of the foods in your meal, and you'll create excitement, eye appeal and appetite!

Let colors accent each other. Combine a multi-colored salad with a main dish that is mainly one color. Or, add colorful garnishes to otherwise plain dishes. You might even want to bring in extra color with cheerful placemats or napkins. Make your meals treats for the eye, as well as for the taste.

Take shape into consideration and incorporate variety on the plate. Foods of different shapes and sizes add a visual interest to a combination of dishes. Round foods such as meatballs would be attractively served with foods of other shapes and sizes, like whole green beans and mashed potatoes.

Let flavors compliment each other. Combine tart, sweet and spicy foods with more bland-flavored ones for balance. Avoid repeating flavors that have been featured in another dish; bring in other different ones instead. Play textures against each other by serving crisp salads and crunchy toppings with some of the softer textures. A saucy main dish goes well with a plain vegetable, and vice versa. Don't forget raw fruits and vegetables for adding a crunch to your meals.

Temperature, too, is a part of the picture. Cold and hot foods make great plate-mates together. Serve a cool, refreshing dessert after a heavy, hot meal. Plan with the weather outside in mind too. Hot, hearty meals taste great on cold days!

"PLANNED-OVER" CREATIVITY

Another way to get the most from your food dollar is to avoid wasteful leftovers. Estimate the number of servings you will need. Then choose a recipe that suits your needs. We've given recipes that serve from 4 to 10 people and have included tips on halving recipes for smaller families. These can be useful guidelines for preparing the appropriate number of serving and avoiding unused leftovers.

But leftovers don't necessarily have to be wasteful ones. We like to think of leftovers as "planned-overs". If you anticipate food which might not be eaten, you can plan a use for it at a later date — a "planned-over". Leftovers from dishes that freeze well (see the Tips following each recipe) can be put in airtight containers or freezer bags and frozen. They make handy lunches and can be a real convenience for unplanned suppers.

We've also included recipes in which "planned-overs" can be used. Since leftovers from roasts are fairly common, we've placed the "planned-over" recipes immediately following the recipes for the various roasts.

Hearty main dish salads are another clever way to use "planned-overs" — especially for quick, casual suppers or hot summer days. These recipes are grouped together in the Meat Salads Chapter.

Leftovers can be disguised in many other ways, too. Add chopped meats to your favorite soups for a hearty lunch or supper idea. Cut leftover roasts into thin slices for sandwiches or cold cut trays. Arrange chunks of leftover meats on a skewer, coat with barbecue sauce, and grill as kabobs. Serve chunks of meat on toothpicks in a spicy sauce for hors d'oeuvres.

Casseroles are also a convenient way to use "planned-overs". You'll find some recipes for casseroles following the kind of meat which the recipe uses. These are only a beginning. Use your creativity to put together great combinations that use the ingredients you have on hand. A wide variety of canned soups, prepared sauces, and mixes for soups and sauces gives you a lot of lee-way. Plan to combine your leftover meats, a vegetable, cooked rice or noodles, and a sauce into a "planned-over", money-stretching meal. Top it with an attractive garnish — crushed potato chips, buttered bread crumbs, grated cheese, paprika, pimiento, sliced olives — and bake at 325° to 350° until vegetables are tender and casserole is heated through.

Casserole combinations or meats with sauces that are thickened with flour or that contain much oil or fat may show some separation after defrosting. Excess fat or oil can be spooned off. Stirring immediately before serving can help the sauce to stay well-blended.

COOKING FOR SMALL FAMILIES

Cooking meat for two or three can be a real challenge, especially since many cuts of meat are sold with larger families in mind. To help meet this problem, we've included Tips for halving, which are located after many of the recipes.

Other recipes, too, can be conveniently cut in half. When recipes call for an entire can of soup, sauce, etc., select another recipe — maybe with a different type of meat — which can use the remaining half. Or, thin the remaining soup to make a sauce or a single portion of soup for lunch or snack.

Roasts and pot-roasts cook with the best flavor if they are at least 3 lbs. in weight. These provide you with a good opportunity to use creative "planned-overs" — either from recipes in this book or ideas of your own. If you freeze portions for later use, take the guesswork out of thawing by labeling according to the amount and type of meat.

Because many meat retailers prepackage their cuts of meat, it is sometimes inconvenient or not possible to purchase quantities for just two or three people. Rewrap the meat at home in quantities which you can conveniently use; refrigerate or freeze for convenience. Freezers are a great help!

Whether your meals are for two or ten, we hope you'll enjoy using the recipes and suggestions in this book. Healthful food and pleasant feelings create a warm and friendly mealtime atmosphere.

Rolled Rib Roast, opposite page

Beef

More meat is produced in the United States than in any other country, and its citizens consume almost the entire amount. Beef, which has been used for food for many centuries, is the most widely and frequently consumed meat — from steaks and roasts to ground beef.

The typical cuts of beef as we know them today have evolved over many years, as special occasions have stimulated new ideas. Some cuts — such as New York Steaks, Porterhouse Steaks, Delmonico Roasts — still bear names relating to their origin or their originator. Sirloin, for example, reportedly got its name when a European king honored the succulent flavor of this cut by royally dubbing it as "Sir Loin".

Beef is produced throughout the United States and is available in a large variety of cuts. They can all be tender and delicious when cooked properly. The recipes in this chapter have been grouped according to the cuts of beef which they use.

When selecting cuts of beef, keep in mind the cooking method or adapt the cooking method to the cut selected. Tender cuts can be cooked to rare or well done; less tender cuts (unless pre-tendered) need to be tenderized by marinating or by long, slow cooking with liquid.

High quality beef should have abundant marbling of fat throughout the lean tissue, should be fine textured and light red to deep red in color, and should have smooth, white fat and red, porous bones.

ROASTS (cooked without liquid)

Standing Rib Roast: A roast containing the back bone, the rib bones, tender muscles from the rib area, and an outer fat covering. For easy carving, have your meat man loosen the back-bone and tie the roast. In restaurants it's served as "Prime Rib".

Standing rib roast is especially nice for carving and serving at the table. Plan your timing so it will be just at the right degree of doneness when ready to serve.

STANDING BEEF RIB ROAST

Standing rib roast
Salt
Pepper

OVEN 325°   ALLOW ¾ TO 1 LB. PER SERVING

Season roast with salt and pepper. Place roast, fat side up, on rack in open shallow roasting pan. Insert meat thermometer so the bulb reaches the center of the largest muscle, being sure that the bulb does not rest in fat or on bone. (Do not add water; do not cover.) Roast at 325° to desired degree of doneness.

Rolled Rib Roast: A Standing Rib Roast which has had the bones removed and has been rolled and tied.

Time this delicious roast carefully so it will be at the desired doneness when ready to serve. Delicious on rotisserie, too.

ROLLED RIB ROAST

Rolled rib roast or rib eye roast
Salt
Pepper

OVEN 325°   ALLOW ¾ TO 1 LB. PER SERVING

Season roast with salt and pepper. Place roast, fat side up, on rack in open shallow roasting pan. Insert meat thermometer so bulb reaches center of thickest part. (Do not add water; do not cover.) Roast at 325° to desired degree of doneness. For ease in carving, let stand 15 minutes. To serve, cut across grain into slices.

How To Carve

Place the roast on the platter with the largest end down to form a solid base. Insert the fork between the two top ribs. Starting on the fat side, carve across the grain to the rib bone.

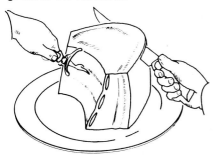

Use the tip of the knife to cut along the rib bone to loosen the slice. Be sure to keep close to the bone, to make the largest servings possible.

Slide the knife back under the slice and, steadying it with the fork, lift the slice to the side of the platter. If the platter is not large enough, place the slices on a heated platter close by.

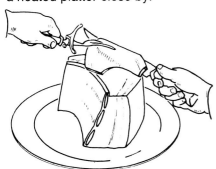

Rib Eye Roast: The large, meaty muscle from the Rib Roast with the outer fat covering and bones removed. It is sometimes referred to as Delmonico Roast. When cut across the grain into sections, it is known as Rib Eye Steak.

For roasts that brown nicely, place roast slightly lower than the center in the oven.

Because of heat retained in the meat, roasts will continue to cook even after they are removed from the oven. Allow for this by cooking roasts to an internal temperature 5 to 10° below the desired final temperature. Allow meat to stand about 15 minutes before carving and serving.

Some of the less tender roasts can be purchased pretendered and can be roasted like the more tender cuts.

TIMETABLE FOR ROASTING BEEF ROASTS

Weight	Doneness	Meat Thermometer Reading	Approx. Cooking Time per Lb.
4 to 6 lbs.	rare	140°	26-32 min.
	medium	160°	34-38 min.
	well	170°	40-42 min.
6 to 8 lbs.	rare	140°	23-25 min.
	medium	160°	27-30 min.
	well	170°	32-35 min.

Tips: Boneless rolled rump and sirloin tip roasts of high quality can be roasted as above. Roast at 325° until medium to well done, allowing 25 to 30 minutes per lb. for rump roast and 35 to 40 minutes per lb. for sirloin tip.

To prepare on rotisserie, follow instructions with oven or grill rotisserie, using a meat thermometer to assure desired degree of doneness. Time will vary from 3 to 5 hours depending on size and shape of cut, temperature when cooking begins and the heat maintained during cooking.

Tenderloin is the tenderest part of beef. Although it is expensive, there is no bone and little fat. It's ready to serve within an hour.

ROAST WHOLE BEEF TENDERLOIN

    4 to 6 lbs. whole beef
        tenderloin
    Salt
    Pepper

OVEN 425°   8 TO 10 SERVINGS

Remove excess surface fat and connective tissue from tenderloin; place on rack in open shallow roasting pan. Turn thin ends under. Brush with oil. Insert meat thermometer so the bulb reaches the center of the thickest part. (Do not add water; do not cover.) Roast at 425° for 45 to 60 minutes until meat thermometer registers 140°. To serve, cut across grain into slices.

Tip: For 4 to 5 servings, roast half a beef tenderloin, as directed, for 45 to 50 minutes.

A tasty mushroom stuffing adds flavor and interest to a rolled rib or rump roast. Buy ½ to ¾ lb. of meat per serving. Serve with oven-browned potatoes, broccoli with cheese sauce and crisp salad.

STUFFED ROLLED ROAST

    1 cup soft bread cubes
    1 cup (8 oz. or 1 pt.) chopped
        fresh or canned mushrooms
    ¼ cup (1 small) chopped
        onion or 1 clove garlic,
        minced
    1 teaspoon salt
    1 teaspoon Worcestershire
        sauce
    Dash pepper
    2 tablespoons red wine or
        water
    2½ to 3½ lbs. rolled rib roast*

OVEN 325°   6 TO 8 SERVINGS

In small mixing bowl, combine all ingredients except roast; mix well. Unroll roast; spread with stuffing mixture. Reroll and tie securely. Place roast on rack in open shallow roasting pan. Insert meat thermometer so the bulb reaches the center portion of meat being sure the bulb does not rest in stuffing. (Do not add water; do not cover.) Roast at 325° to the desired degree of doneness, using timetable for Rolled Rib Roast. If desired, make gravy from pan drippings. For ease in carving, let stand 15 minutes. To serve, cut across grain into slices.

Tip: *A rolled rump roast can be used; however, it should be of a high quality to assure tender meat. It may be necessary to make an additional cut in the meat to allow space for the stuffing. Roast at 325° until medium to well done, allowing 25 to 30 minutes per lb.

TIMETABLE FOR ROASTING BEEF ROASTS

Weight	Doneness	Meat Thermometer Reading	Approx. Cooking Time per Lb.
4 to 6 lbs.	rare	140°	26-32 min.
	medium	160°	34-38 min.
	well	170°	40-42 min.
6 to 8 lbs.	rare	140°	23-25 min.
	medium	160°	27-30 min.
	well	170°	32-35 min.

Sirloin Tip: A small tip of the sirloin is included in this roast from the round steak area. If it is from high quality meat, it can be roasted just like some of the more tender cuts.

Heel of Round: This wedge-shaped or triangular cut is from the end of the round steak (rump) area where there is no bone. It is less tender than the Rump Roast and should be cooked with liquid unless it has been pretendered.

Marinate the meat 24 hours for a milder flavored sauerbraten; 48 hours if you like a stronger flavor. Ginger-snaps make a quick and flavorful thickening.

SAUERBRATEN

   3 to 3½ lbs. heel of round, rump or sirloin tip roast
   1 cup red wine vinegar
1½ cups water
   1 onion, sliced
   1 stalk celery, sliced
   5 whole cloves
   2 bay leaves
   1 tablespoon (3 tsp.) salt
   4 peppercorns or ¼ teaspoon pepper
   2 tablespoons oil or shortening
   2 tablespoons brown sugar
   6 gingersnaps, crushed

6 TO 8 SERVINGS

Place meat in glass bowl. Add remaining ingredients except oil, brown sugar and gingersnaps. Cover and marinate in refrigerator 24 to 48 hours, turning meat several times to season evenly. Remove meat from marinade; drain well. In Dutch oven, brown meat in hot oil on all sides. Add 1½ cups of strained marinade. Cover and simmer 2½ to 3 hours until tender. Remove meat to heated platter. Spoon fat off of juices. Add brown sugar and gingersnaps to juices. Cook, stirring constantly, until mixture comes to a boil. If necessary, thin with water or remaining marinade. Pour over meat. Serve with potato pancakes, potato dumplings or boiled potatoes.

Leftover beef, potatoes and gravy — here's an easy and delicious way to serve them. Dinner can be ready in 30 minutes.

OLD FASHIONED HASH

   3 cups diced cooked beef
   3 cups diced cooked potatoes
   ½ cup (1 med.) chopped onion
   ½ cup leftover gravy or cream soup
   ½ to 1 teaspoon salt
   ⅛ teaspoon pepper
   2 tablespoons catsup
   ½ teaspoon prepared mustard
   2 tablespoons oil or shortening

5 TO 6 SERVINGS

In large bowl, combine all ingredients except oil. In large fry pan, heat oil; add hash. Cook over medium heat until well browned about 10 minutes. Turn and brown other side.

Tip: For 2 to 3 servings, halve all ingredients. Prepare as directed.

Dress up leftover beef roast in a stroganoff sauce, made easy with canned soup.

BEEF IN SOUR CREAM SAUCE

   3 to 4 cups cubed cooked beef
1¼ cups (10½-oz. can) condensed cream of mushroom or celery soup
   ½ cup (4-oz. can) drained mushroom stems and pieces
   ¼ cup water or mushroom liquid
   ½ cup dairy sour cream

4 TO 5 SERVINGS

In fry pan or saucepan, combine all ingredients except sour cream. Simmer about 15 minutes. Stir in sour cream; heat through. Serve over rice or noodles.

Tips: If desired, use golden mushroom soup and omit water.

Leftover gravy can be used for soup; omit water, unless mixture seems too thick.

Dress up leftover beef roast with a spicy barbecue sauce. Start about 1 hour ahead; serve with potato chips and a salad.

Leftover roast reappears as a quick-to-make beef stew. For a heartier meal, top with favorite dumplings or refrigerated biscuits during last 20 minutes of cooking.

BARBECUED SLICED BEEF

1½ cups (2 med.) chopped onions
2 tablespoons butter or margarine
1½ cups catsup
¼ cup firmly packed brown sugar
¼ cup lemon juice or vinegar
2 teaspoons dry or 1 tablespoon prepared mustard
1½ teaspoons salt
¼ teaspoon pepper
⅛ teaspoon ground cloves
1 tablespoon Worcestershire sauce
12 thin slices cooked beef
6 hamburger buns

6 SERVINGS

In fry pan, sauté onions in butter until golden. Add catsup, brown sugar, lemon juice, mustard, salt, pepper, cloves and Worcestershire sauce. Simmer 30 minutes. Add beef; simmer 15 minutes longer. Serve on warm buns.

Tip: For 3 servings, halve all ingredients. Prepare as directed.

QUICK BEEF AND VEGETABLE STEW

4 cups cubed cooked beef (1-inch cubes)
1¼ cups (10½-oz. can) condensed golden mushroom soup
¾ cup water
1 onion, quartered
3 carrots, cut into 1-inch pieces
3 potatoes, cut into 1-inch cubes
1½ cups (10-oz. pkg.) frozen peas, if desired

4 TO 6 SERVINGS

In large saucepan, combine all ingredients except peas. Simmer, covered, for 20 minutes; add peas and continue cooking for 15 minutes until all vegetables are tender.

Tip: If desired, use 1 envelope dry onion soup mix for golden mushroom soup; increase water to 2 cups.

Use other vegetables, too; also try with leftover vegetables — just add them 5 to 10 minutes before serving.

Sauerbraten, opposite page, with Red Cabbage and Potato Dumplings

Pot-Roast in Foil, opposite page

POT-ROASTS (cooked with liquid)

Blade Bone Roast: This cut is really a pot-roast and includes several meat muscles, the blade bone and sometimes part of the backbone. Cut from the shoulder (chuck) area near the rib section, it is usually less expensive than arm bone roasts, contains slightly more bone and waste, and is sometimes referred to as Chuck Roast. Occasionally it is boned, rolled and tied and called Boneless Chuck Pot Roast. If cut into 1 to 2-inch slices, it is called Blade Steak.

OVEN BAKED POT-ROAST

3 to 4 lbs. chuck (arm or blade) pot-roast
½ cup (1 envelope) dry onion soup mix
3 to 4 medium potatoes, cut into quarters
4 carrots, cut into quarters
1 large stalk celery, cut into pieces

OVEN 350°   6 TO 8 SERVINGS

Place pot-roast in baking dish or casserole with cover. Sprinkle onion soup mix over meat. Cover; bake at 350° for 2 to 2½ hours. Add potatoes, carrots and celery; cover and continue baking for 1 hour.

Arm Bone Roast: This cut contains the arm bone and sometimes cross sections of the rib bones — unless they are removed by the retailer — and is from the shoulder (chuck) area. You can tell it from the round steak because the bone is nearer the center of the cut and includes several small meat muscles. It is sometimes called Chuck Roast. If cut into 1 to 1½-inch slices, it is called Arm Steak.

POT-ROAST IN FOIL

3 to 4 lbs. chuck (arm or blade) pot-roast
½ cup (1 envelope) dry onion soup mix

OVEN 350°   6 TO 8 SERVINGS

Place meat in center of a piece of heavy duty foil; sprinkle with dry soup mix. Bring edges of foil together and seal with double fold; seal ends with double fold. Place seam-side up in shallow baking pan. Bake at 350° for 2½ to 3 hours until meat is tender.

Tip: For variety, add one of the following along with soup: sliced fresh or canned mushrooms, sliced celery, sliced carrots or green pepper rings.

BEEF POT-ROAST WITH VEGETABLES

3 to 3½ lbs. chuck (arm or blade) or rump pot-roast
1 tablespoon oil or shortening
2½ cups water
2 teaspoons salt
¼ teaspoon pepper
1 bay leaf
4 medium onions, sliced
3 stalks celery, cut into pieces
6 medium carrots, cut into pieces
4 medium potatoes, cut in half

6 SERVINGS

Brown pot-roast on both sides in oil in heavy fry pan or Dutch oven for about 15 minutes. Add water, salt, pepper, bay leaf, 1 onion and 1 stalk celery. Cover tightly and simmer 2 to 2½ hours until meat is tender. Add vegetables; simmer 45 to 60 minutes until tender. Remove meat and vegetables to heated platter. If desired, thicken juice with 3 tablespoons flour that has been mixed with ¼ cup water. Stir into liquid in pan. Cook, stirring constantly, until mixture comes to a boil. Serve with meat.

Tips: Part red wine (about 1 cup) may be used for part of water.

Use other vegetables, too: rutabagas, mushrooms or cabbage wedges.

For easy pot-roast, omit salt, pepper and first addition of onion and celery; add 1 envelope dry onion soup mix with water.

To make ahead, prepare except for adding vegetables; cool and refrigerate or freeze. To serve, reheat, add vegetables and simmer 45 minutes.

For 2 to 3 servings, halve all ingredients. Prepare as directed.

For a different twist to pot-roast, try this recipe with a barbecue sauce. Plan it around your schedule — start 2¼ hours ahead, or prepare partially the night before. Serve with baked potatoes and asparagus or other green vegetables.

OVEN BARBECUED POT-ROAST

· 3 to 3½ lbs. chuck (arm or blade) pot-roast

Barbecue Sauce

   1 cup (8-oz. can) tomato
     sauce
  ¼ cup red wine or water
   2 tablespoons brown sugar
  ½ teaspoon salt
   2 teaspoons prepared or
     1 teaspoon dry mustard
   1 clove garlic, minced or
     ⅛ teaspoon instant minced
     garlic or garlic powder
   1 medium onion, sliced
  ½ lemon, sliced

OVEN 350°   6 TO 8 SERVINGS

In large saucepan, cover roast with water; salt to taste. Simmer, covered, over medium low heat 1½ hours (meanwhile prepare Barbecue Sauce). Drain; place roast in baking dish. Pour Barbecue Sauce over, coating roast well. Cover tightly with lid or foil. Bake at 350° for 45 to 60 minutes until tender.

Barbecue Sauce: Combine all ingredients.

Tips: For a quick Barbecue Sauce, use 1 cup of your favorite prepared barbecue sauce, adding mustard, garlic, onion and lemon.

To reheat, add a little water; cover and reheat at 325° for about 30 minutes.

To make ahead, pour Barbecue Sauce over partially cooked meat in baking dish; cool, cover and refrigerate. Bake at 350° for about 1 hour until meat is tender and heated through.

This dish freezes well after cooking. Add a little water before reheating.

An easy pot-roast made with mushroom soup. Start 3 hours ahead and let it simmer until time to serve. Serve with a colorful vegetable and crisp salad.

POT-ROAST WITH MUSHROOM GRAVY

   3 lb. chuck (arm or blade) or
     rump pot-roast
   2 tablespoons oil or
     shortening
   1 large onion, sliced
  ½ cup red wine or water
  ¼ cup water
   2 teaspoons garlic salt
   1 teaspoon paprika
  ⅛ teaspoon pepper
   1 tablespoon Worcestershire
     sauce
  1¼ cups (10½-oz. can) con-
     densed cream of mushroom
     soup

          6 SERVINGS

Brown meat on both sides in oil in Dutch oven or large fry pan. Stir in remaining ingredients. Cover tightly. Simmer 2½ to 3 hours until tender. Skim off fat; serve sauce over meat along with potatoes or rice.

Tip: To make ahead, prepare, cool and refrigerate or freeze. Reheat and serve, thinning with additional water if necessary.

Beef Brisket: This cut contains the breast bone and portions of the ribs, although it is frequently boned and sold as Boneless Brisket. It comes from the breast and rib area and requires long simmering in liquid for tenderness.

Perfect fare for a cold, winter day. Start cooking 4 hours ahead.

NEW ENGLAND BOILED DINNER

   3 lbs. corned beef
   1 bay leaf
   1 teaspoon peppercorns
   6 potatoes, quartered
   6 carrots, cut in half
     lengthwise
   6 wedges cabbage
  1½ cups (10-oz. pkg.) frozen
     peas, if desired

          6 SERVINGS

In large saucepan, cover corned beef with water. Add bay leaf and peppercorns. Cover and simmer over low heat 3 to 3½ hours until tender. Add potatoes and carrots. Cover and simmer 15 minutes. Add cabbage and peas. Cook 15 minutes longer until vegetables are tender. Cut meat in pieces. Serve some of broth along with vegetables.

Tips: To make ahead, cook corned beef; remove bay leaf and refrigerate or freeze. Reheat and add vegetables, continuing as directed.

For less than 6 servings, cook meat as directed and add less vegetables. Serve leftover corned beef in sandwiches.

Corned Beef Brisket: Meat from the less tender brisket area (breast and rib) that has been cured. Long, slow simmering with liquid is required unless this cut has been pre-tendered. (If the cut has not been cured, it is sold as fresh Beef Brisket. The word "corned" refers to the curing which gives the distinct "corned beef" flavor.)

New England Boiled Dinner, opposite page, see Tip

STEAKS (tender)

T-bone Steak: The bone, which has the distinct T shape, separates the large loin muscle from the small tenderloin muscle. This cut comes from the loin area.

Rib Steak: The rib bone identifies this cut easily. It is cut from the rib area — similar to the Rib Roast, only cut into 1 to 2-inch thick steaks. If it is sold without bone or outside fat trimming, it is called Rib Eye Steak.

Tenderloin Steak: This cross-section of the tenderloin muscle has no bone and very little fat. It is also sold as Filet Mignon.

Sirloin Steak: A large, tender steak that contains several large muscles. It may be boneless or may contain a small wedge or flat bone. The top (largest) muscle is sometimes separated and sold as Top Sirloin Steak.

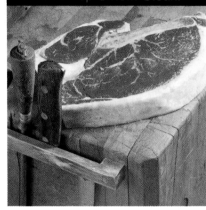

Broiling times vary according to:
    Type of heat used
    Distance from the heat
    Thickness of meat
    Whether broiler is preheated
    or not
Consult your operator's manual for specific directions.

Club Steak: This steak is similar to the Rib Steak, but sometimes includes a small portion of the tenderloin muscle. It is cut from the rib area and may or may not contain a rib bone.

To prevent steaks from curling during cooking, slash the fat edge at 1 to 2-inch intervals, without cutting through the lean tissue.

Timetable for Broiling

Steak	Thickness	Approx. Total Cooking Time	
		Rare	Medium
Rib, rib eye or club steak	1 inch	15 min.	20 min.
	1½ inches	25 min.	30 min.
	2 inches	35 min.	45 min.
Sirloin, porterhouse, or T-bone steak	1 inch	20 min.	25 min.
	1½ inches	30 min.	35 min.
	2 inches	40 min.	45 min.

Select a tender, good quality steak for broiling — rib, rib eye, club, sirloin, porterhouse or T-bone. Allow ¾ to 1 lb. per serving with a bone; ½ to ¾ lb. per serving for boneless steak.

BROILED STEAK

Set regulator for broiling. Place steak on broiler rack. Insert broiler pan and rack so the top of 1-inch steak is 2 to 3 inches from the heat and 2-inch steak is 3 to 5 inches from the heat. When one side is browned, season with salt and pepper, then turn and finish cooking (see timetable below) on the second side. Season with salt and pepper.

An easy to prepare company meal if you prepare the meat, vegetables and soy sauce mixture early; then cover and refrigerate. Just start cooking 15 minutes before serving time.

SUKIYAKI

1 to 1½ lbs. sirloin tip or sirloin steak
2 tablespoons oil or shortening
½ cup soy sauce
⅔ cup water
3 tablespoons sugar
½ teaspoon MSG (monosodium glutamate), if desired
¾ cup (5-oz. can) drained bamboo shoots
1 cup green onions, cut into 1-inch pieces
2 medium onions, thinly sliced
2 cups (1-lb. can) drained bean sprouts
⅔ cup (5-oz. can) sliced water chestnuts
1 cup (8 oz. or ½ pt.) sliced fresh or canned mushrooms

4 TO 6 SERVINGS

Cut meat into paper-thin slices across the grain, (freezing meat makes slicing easier) then into strips 1-inch wide. Brown strips in hot oil in large fry pan 2 to 3 minutes. Combine soy sauce, water, sugar and MSG. Pour over meat. Push meat to one side of fry pan. Keeping the ingredients separate, add bamboo shoots, green onions and onion slices. Cook 5 to 10 minutes, turning vegetables and keeping separate. Push vegetables to one side. Add bean sprouts, water chestnuts and mushrooms, keeping ingredients separate. Cook 2 minutes until hot. Serve with rice.

Tip: An electric fry pan set at 400° to 425° can be used to cook Sukiyaki.

Use round steak (see Tip) for a tempting family dish or sirloin steak to serve with a flair in your chafing dish. Serve over rice along with a buttered green vegetable and a cool refreshing salad.

BEEF STROGANOFF

2 lbs. sirloin steak, cut into thin strips
2 cups (16 oz. or 1 pt.) sliced fresh mushrooms
2 medium onions, sliced
2 tablespoons oil or shortening
3 beef bouillon cubes
1 cup water
½ teaspoon salt
2 tablespoons tomato paste or catsup
1 teaspoon dry or prepared mustard
2 tablespoons flour
½ cup cold water
½ to 1 cup dairy sour cream

6 SERVINGS

In large fry pan, sauté steak, mushrooms and onions in hot oil until golden brown. Add bouillon cubes, water, salt, tomato paste and mustard. Cover; simmer 30 to 45 minutes until tender. Combine flour and cold water. Slowly stir into meat mixture. Cook, stirring constantly, until mixture comes to a boil. Reduce heat. Stir in sour cream. Heat, but do not boil. Serve over rice or noodles.

Tips: If desired, use round or family steak, cut into thin strips; add 1¼ cups hot water and simmer 1 to 1½ hours until meat is tender.

Red wine can be used for half of hot water addition.

To make ahead, prepare except for adding sour cream. Reheat and add sour cream when ready to serve.

This recipe can be frozen for up to 2 weeks. Reheat, covered, in oven or in saucepan.

For 2 to 3 servings, halve all ingredients. Prepare as directed.

Beef Bourguignonne, opposite page

Red wine and beef cubes blend perfectly for this oven dish. Start about 1¼ hours before serving — add buttered carrots and a molded fruit salad to complete your menu.

BEEF BOURGUIGNONNE

- 2 tablespoons oil or shortening
- 2 lbs. sirloin steak, cut into 1½-inch cubes
- 1 medium green pepper, cut into 2-inch pieces
- 1 cup (8 oz. or ½ pt.) sliced or quartered fresh mushrooms
- 2 tablespoons chopped onion or ½ teaspoon instant minced onion
- 2 tablespoons flour
- 1 teaspoon salt
- ⅔ cup dry red wine
- 1⅔ cups (1-lb. can) drained, whole onions

OVEN 400°   4 TO 6 SERVINGS

Place oil in 2½-quart casserole. Add steak, green pepper, mushrooms and onion. Bake, uncovered, at 400° for 30 minutes, stirring occasionally. Remove from oven, stir in flour and salt. Blend in wine and whole onions. Cover and bake 30 minutes longer. Serve over noodles or rice.

Use scissors to cut meat into strips, cubes or sections.

Use your fondue pot for cooking this typical Chinese dish. Arrange the meats, fish and vegetables on a pretty tray; then, let each guest cook his own in the hot chicken broth.

CHINESE HOT POT FONDUE

- 2 chicken breasts, skinned, boned and cut into thin strips
- ½ lb. boneless beef sirloin, cut into thin strips
- 1½ cups (7 oz.) fresh or frozen* shrimp
- 2 cups fresh spinach or sliced Chinese cabbage
- 2 cups (8 oz. or 1 pt.) fresh mushrooms
- ½ head cauliflower divided into small pieces
- 6 cups chicken broth**
- 2 teaspoons salt

4 SERVINGS

Prepare chicken, beef, shrimp and vegetables; arrange on serving tray. Cover and refrigerate until time to serve. Prepare desired sauces. (Use bottled soy sauce, sweet and sour sauce, mustard sauce, teriyaki sauce or prepare your own — see recipes that follow.) Heat chicken broth and salt until bubbly. Pour into fondue pot; place over heating unit in center of table. Set out dishes of sauces. Each guest uses fondue fork to spear piece of vegetable and/or meat and cooks it in the hot chicken broth. Serve with rice (use a covered dish or warming tray to keep warm throughout meal) and sauces. From time to time, spoon some of chicken broth over rice or pass additional broth.

Tips: *Frozen shrimp can be just thawed and set out; however, they lack the pretty pink color. For more attractive shrimp, dip into boiling water just until pink and firm.

**For chicken broth, use broth from stewed chicken or the canned chicken broth — use enough to fill fondue pot about ⅔ full. If desired, use 1 cup

white wine or sherry for 1 cup of chicken broth.

If desired, ½ lb. lamb, cut into thin strips, and 1 eggplant, cut into ½-inch cubes, can be used for the beef and cauliflower.

TERIYAKI SAUCE:

½ CUP SAUCE

In small saucepan, combine 2 teaspoons cornstarch with 1 teaspoon ground ginger, ¼ cup white wine and ¼ cup soy sauce. Cook over medium heat, stirring constantly, until thickened; serve warm.

CREAMY MUSTARD SAUCE:

½ CUP SAUCE

Combine ½ cup plain yogurt or dairy sour cream with 1½ table-spoons prepared mustard and a few drops of Tabasco sauce. Refrigerate until served.

SWEET AND SOUR SAUCE:

1 CUP SAUCE

In small saucepan, combine ½ cup firmly packed brown sugar with 1 tablespoon cornstarch, ½ teaspoon salt, ½ teaspoon paprika, ½ cup pineapple juice and ¼ cup vinegar. Cook over medium heat, stirring constantly, until thickened; serve warm.

STEAKS (less tender)

Round Steak: This steak may have the characteristic round bone with 1 large muscle above the bone (often separated and sold as Top Round) and 2 smaller muscles below the bone (often separated and sold as Bottom Round). The smallest muscle is occasionally separated and sold as Eye of Round Steak. Family Steak and Swiss Steak are usually cut from this same rump area. Unless pretendered, they should be cooked with liquid.

Chuck Steak: Chuck Steak is similar to Chuck Roast, except that it is cut 1 to 2-inches thick. It usually contains the blade bone (see Blade Pot-Roast, page 23) or arm bone (see Arm Pot-Roast, page 23). This steak is from the shoulder area. ("Chuck" is another term for shoulder and is associated with pot-roasts.) It is sometimes sold as Barbecue Steak; but unless pretenderized, it must be tenderized before grilling.

Family Steak: This steak is cut differently in various parts of the country. It is usually cut from the round (pictured here), chuck or sirloin area. Family steak is often recommended for barbecuing, but we suggest some type of marinating or tenderizing before grilling or broiling — especially if it is from the round or chuck area.

Carrots, onion and celery add flavor and color when rolled up in pieces of round steak. Ready to serve in 1¾ hours along with potatoes and salad — or see Tip for starting the night before.

VEGETABLE BEEF ROLL-UPS

  1½ to 2 lbs. round steak
    2 tablespoons flour
    1 teaspoon salt
    ⅛ teaspoon pepper
    3 carrots
    3 stalks celery
    1 medium onion, cut into
      6 wedges
    2 tablespoons oil or
      shortening
    1 cup water or combination
      of red wine and water

             6 SERVINGS

Cut steak into 6 pieces. Combine flour, salt and pepper. Pound meat with meat hammer or edge of heavy saucer, coating with flour mixture and pounding both sides. Cut carrots and celery in half and then in quarters. Place wedge of onion, 2 carrot sticks and 2 celery sticks on each piece of meat. Roll up and fasten with toothpicks. Brown in hot oil in fry pan. Add water. Cover tightly. Simmer 1½ hours until tender. Remove meat to heated platter. Make gravy from pan drippings or add ½ to 1 can of condensed cream of tomato, mushroom or celery soup to pan drippings; heat and serve over steak.

Tip: To make ahead, prepare except for gravy. Cool, refrigerate or freeze. Reheat, adding water if necessary. Prepare gravy as directed.

Swiss steak with an easy sauce made from tomato soup. Begin 2 hours ahead; serve with boiled potatoes and a crisp lettuce wedge.

SWISS STEAK

    2 to 2½ lbs. round, Swiss or
      family steak
    ¼ cup flour
    2 tablespoons oil or
      shortening
    1 teaspoon salt
    ⅛ teaspoon pepper
    ⅔ cup (4-oz. can) undrained
      mushroom stems and
      pieces
    1 large onion, sliced or
      ¼ cup instant minced onion
  1¼ cups (10½-oz. can)
      condensed cream of
      tomato soup
  1½ cups (10-oz. pkg.) frozen
      peas, if desired

OVEN 350°   6 SERVINGS

Cut steak into 6 pieces. Coat with flour. Brown on both sides in hot oil in large fry pan. Sprinkle with salt and pepper. Add mushrooms and liquid, onion and soup. Cover tightly. Simmer on top of range or bake at 350° for 1½ to 2 hours, adding peas during last 20 minutes of cooking.

Tip: To make ahead, simmer for about 1 hour; cool and refrigerate or freeze. Simmer ½ to 1 hour more before serving.

Swiss Steak, opposite page

Individual steak rolls come to dinner with sherry stuffing and a mushroom-almond sauce. Allow three hours, then serve with mashed potatoes, Brussels sprouts and a cool molded salad.

CONTINENTAL STEAK ROLLS

    2 cups soft bread cubes
    ¼ cup chopped ripe olives, if
        desired
    ⅓ cup cooking sherry or beef
        bouillon
    1 teaspoon onion salt
    1 teaspoon Worcestershire
        sauce
    ¼ teaspoon pepper
    2 lbs. round steak, cut
        ½-inch thick
    ¼ cup flour
    ½ teaspoon salt
    ½ teaspoon garlic salt
    ¼ cup slivered almonds
    1¼ cups (10½-oz. can)
        condensed cream of
        mushroom soup
    ½ cup milk
    ⅛ teaspoon ground nutmeg

OVEN 350°   6 SERVINGS

Combine bread cubes, olives, sherry, onion salt, Worcestershire sauce and pepper. Cut round steak into 6 serving pieces. Coat with mixture of flour, salt and garlic salt. Top each with 1/6 of stuffing. Bring opposite edges around stuffing to meet. Fasten with toothpicks. Place seam-side down in greased shallow 2-quart casserole. Sprinkle with almonds. Bake, uncovered, at 350° for 30 minutes. Remove from oven. Combine soup, milk and nutmeg. Pour over steak rolls. Cover and bake 2 hours longer until meat is tender. Serve with sauce. If desired, garnish with fresh snipped parsley.

Tips: To make ahead, prepare meat rolls, with stuffing. Cover and refrigerate. Begin cooking 2½ to 3 hours before serving.

Or, make and cook ahead; refrigerate or freeze; then, reheat to serve.

A delicious flavored sauce combines with round steak to simmer to a luscious tenderness. Served over noodles or by itself, all this dish needs to make a great meal is a vegetable and a salad.

SUPERB SWISS STEAK

    2½ to 3 lbs. Swiss steak or
        round steak
    1 teaspoon seasoned salt
    ¼ teaspoon pepper
    ¼ cup flour
    2 tablespoons cooking oil
    1 cup (8-oz. can) undrained
        tomatoes, cut into pieces
    1 cup (8-oz. can) tomato
        sauce
    1 package (⅝ oz.) Pillsbury
        Brown Gravy Mix
    1 large onion, sliced

            6 TO 8 SERVINGS

Cut meat into serving pieces. Combine seasoned salt, pepper and flour in shallow bowl or plastic bag. Coat meat in seasoned flour. Brown meat in oil in large fry pan; drain excess fat. Add remaining ingredients. Simmer, covered, 1½ to 2 hours until meat is tender. If desired, serve over noodles.

Tip: To make ahead, prepare as directed, simmering until tender. Refrigerate. Heat thoroughly before serving.

A Swiss-type of steak with a Spanish flavor. Serve in 1½ hours with rice, green vegetable, and salad of assorted fruits on lettuce.

SPANISH STEAK

    2 to 2½ lbs. round, Swiss or
        family steak
    ¼ cup flour
    1 teaspoon salt
    ¼ teaspoon pepper
    2 tablespoons oil or
        shortening
    1 onion, sliced
    1 green pepper, sliced
    2 cups (1-lb. can) undrained
        tomatoes
    1 teaspoon chili powder

                6 SERVINGS

Cut steak into 6 pieces. Combine flour, salt and pepper. Coat meat

with seasoned flour. In large fry pan, brown meat on both sides in hot oil. Add onion and green pepper; continue cooking 5 minutes. Add remaining ingredients. Cover; simmer 1 to 1½ hours until tender. Skim off fat and serve sauce with meat.

Tips: To oven cook, place browned steak, onion and green pepper in baking dish or casserole; add remaining ingredients, cover and bake at 350° for 1 to 1½ hours.

To make ahead, simmer about 1 hour. Cool and refrigerate or freeze. Simmer ½ hour more before serving.

For 2 to 3 servings, halve all ingredients. Prepare as directed.

Round steak and mushroom soup are cooked together for an easy, tasty combination. Try other soups, too — golden mushroom, onion, celery or tomato.

STEAK IN MUSHROOM GRAVY

    2 to 2½ lbs. round or family
        steak
    2 tablespoons oil or
        shortening
    1¼ cups (10½ oz. can)
        condensed cream of
        mushroom soup
    1 teaspoon instant minced
        onion or 1 small onion,
        chopped
    1 teaspoon salt
    1 teaspoon Worcestershire
        sauce

            ABOUT 6 SERVINGS

In large fry pan, brown meat in hot oil on both sides. Combine remaining ingredients and pour over meat. Cover; simmer 1½ to 2 hours until meat is tender.

Tips: Meat can be cooked whole or cut into serving pieces.

For 3 servings, halve all ingredients. Prepare as directed.

Subtle onion and tomato flavors give this steak a tantalizing flavor. Peas, a fruit salad and mashed potatoes round out a meal that the whole gang will rave about!

IMPERIAL BEEF

  1½ lbs. round steak
  ¼ cup flour
  1 teaspoon salt
  ¼ teaspoon pepper
  2 tablespoons oil
  1 cup (8-oz. can) drained
    small whole onions,
    reserve ½ cup liquid*
  ⅔ cup (half 10½-oz. can)
    condensed cream of
    mushroom soup
  Reserved ½ cup onion
    liquid
  ¼ cup water
  1 tablespoon catsup

                    6 SERVINGS

Cut meat into serving pieces. Combine flour, salt and pepper; coat meat with flour mixture. Brown meat in oil in large fry pan. Add remaining ingredients. Simmer, covered, about 1½ hours until meat is tender. Serve with sauce.

Tip: *If desired, ¼ cup instant minced onion can be used for the whole onions; add ½ cup water.

Steak rolls with flavorful bacon and onions in the center, baked to tenderness and topped with a white sauce. Serve this favorite with parslied potatoes, a green vegetable and a crisp salad.

BACON-STEAK ROLLS

  1½ lbs. round steak, cut
    ½-inch thick
  ½ teaspoon salt
  ⅛ teaspoon pepper
  5 slices bacon, chopped
  1¼ teaspoon instant minced
    onion or 5 tablespoons
    finely chopped onion
  1 tablespoon cooking oil
  1 cup milk
  2 tablespoons flour

OVEN 350°   5 SERVINGS

Sprinkle meat with salt and pepper. Cut meat into serving pieces. Place about 2 tablespoons chopped bacon and ¼ teaspoon instant minced onion in center of each piece of meat. Roll pieces up and secure with toothpicks. In large fry pan or oven-going pan, brown meat rolls in oil. Bake, covered, at 350° for 1½ hours until steak is tender. Remove steak rolls from fry pan; drain excess fat, reserving meat juices. Combine milk and flour; add slowly to reserved meat juices. Simmer, stirring constantly, until sauce thickens and comes to a boil. Add steak rolls to sauce; simmer 5 minutes. Serve steak rolls with sauce.

An outdoor-flavored dish that you can do in your own kitchen. Start 1½ hours early; serve with your favorite barbecue side dishes.

ROUND STEAK BARBECUE

  1½ to 2 lbs. round steak or
    family steak
  2 tablespoons oil or
    shortening
  ½ cup (1 med.) chopped
    onion or 2 tablespoons
    instant minced onion
  3 tablespoons sugar
  2 teaspoons salt or seasoned
    salt
  3 tablespoons
    Worcestershire sauce
  2 tablespoons prepared
    mustard
  1 cup water
  1 cup (8-oz. can) tomato
    sauce

                  6 TO 8 SERVINGS

Cut meat into serving pieces. Brown meat in oil in large fry pan. Add remaining ingredients; stir to combine. Simmer, stirring occasionally, until sauce thickens and comes to a boil. Simmer, covered, 1¼ to 1½ hours until tender.

Tip: For 3 to 4 servings, halve all ingredients. Prepare as directed.

Dutch ovens, fry pans or casserole dishes that can be used both on top of the range AND in the oven are handy for making casseroles in which the meat is browned before adding the remaining ingredients.

A delicious, tangy sauce covers this meat while it simmers to tenderness. Peas and a crisp lettuce salad complete the meal — a favorite for your family!

SAUCY STEAK SPECIAL

  1½ lbs. round steak or family
    steak
  1 tablespoon cooking oil
  ½ cup (1 med.) chopped
    onion or 2 tablespoons
    instant minced onion
  ⅔ cup (half 10½-oz. can)
    condensed mushroom
    soup*
  ⅔ cup (half 10½-oz. can)
    condensed tomato soup
  ½ cup water
  ¼ cup sherry
  1 tablespoon cornstarch
  2 tablespoons
    Worcestershire sauce
  2 teaspoons soy sauce

                    6 SERVINGS

Cut meat into serving pieces. Brown in oil in large fry pan. Add onion and cook until tender. Stir in mushroom soup, tomato soup, water and sherry. Combine cornstarch with Worcestershire sauce and soy sauce; add to meat mixture. Blend well. Simmer, covered, about 1½ hours until meat is tender. Serve over noodles or rice.

Tip: *If desired, use one entire can of either mushroom or tomato soup instead of the combination.

Try this steak barbecued in a fry pan with a lemon-flavored barbecue sauce. To serve it, cut meat across the grain into ½ -inch slices. Cole-slaw and your favorite vegetable make it a complete meal. See the tip for using oranges instead of lemons.

CITRUS SIMMERED STEAK

1¾ to 2 lbs. round steak, cut 1¾-inches thick
2 tablespoons cooking oil
½ cup (4-oz. can) drained mushroom pieces, if desired

½ cup (1 med.) onion slices
2 tablespoons barbecue sauce or catsup
1 tablespoon lemon juice
1 tablespoon soy sauce
1 teaspoon grated lemon peel
½ teaspoon salt
⅛ teaspoon ground thyme, if desired
¼ cup water
1 tablespoon sugar
1 tablespoon cornstarch
2 lemons, sliced

In large fry pan, brown meat in oil on both sides. Add mushrooms, onions, barbecue sauce, lemon juice, soy sauce, lemon peel, salt and thyme. Simmer, covered, 1½ to 2 hours until meat is tender. Combine water, sugar and cornstarch; stir to blend. Add cornstarch mixture and sliced lemon to meat mixture; stir to blend. Continue simmering until sauce thickens.

Tip: If desired, orange juice, grated orange peel and sliced oranges can be used for the lemon.

*Citrus Simmered Steak.
above, see Tip*

Flank steak makes an economical, flavorful steak, but should be medium rare to assure tenderness. Serve it plain or spoon favorite mushroom sauce over slices. Ready to eat in 15 minutes.

LONDON BROIL

2 to 2½ lbs. flank steak
Meat tenderizer
¼ cup butter or margarine, melted
Pepper

4 TO 6 SERVINGS

Score flank steak on each side at 1-inch intervals. Prepare steak with meat tenderizer as directed on label. Place steak on rack in broiling pan and broil 3 inches from heat for 5 minutes. Brush with butter and season with pepper. Turn and broil 5 minutes longer until medium rare. Brush with remaining butter and season with more pepper. Cut on the diagonal, across grain, into very thin slices.

Tips: For garlic flavor, add clove of garlic to butter when melting.

For 2 servings, halve all ingredients. Prepare as directed. Remaining half of Flank Steak can be frozen or used later in another recipe, such as Teriyaki Steak, page 126.

A deliciously flavored sauce lets this meat simmer to perfection. Corn and a crisp salad can complete the meal. See Tip for make-ahead directions.

PEPPER STEAK

1 flank steak (1½ to 2 lbs.)
¼ cup and 2 tablespoons flour
2 tablespoons oil or shortening
2 green peppers, cut into 1-inch squares
1¼ cups water
1 beef bouillon cube or 1 teaspoon instant bouillon
½ teaspoon salt
⅛ teaspoon pepper
1 clove garlic, crushed

6 SERVINGS

Score flank steak and cut into 6 pieces. Coat with flour. Brown meat on both sides in oil in large fry pan. Add green pepper, water, bouillon cube, salt, pepper and garlic. Cover and simmer 2 hours until tender. Serve over rice or noodles with sauce.

Tip: To make ahead, prepare as directed, omitting green pepper and simmering only 1½ hours. Refrigerate overnight or freeze. When ready to serve, add green pepper and simmer ½ hour until meat is tender.

Strips of flank steak take on an Italian flavor when simmered in this spicy tomato sauce. Serve with a crisp salad and French bread.

FLANK STEAK ITALIANO

1 flank steak (about 1½ lbs.)
1 tablespoon oil or shortening
2 cloves garlic, minced or ¼ teaspoon garlic powder or instant minced garlic
1 tablespoon parsley flakes
½ teaspoon salt
½ teaspoon leaf oregano or Italian seasoning
¼ teaspoon leaf basil
1¼ cups water
1 cup red wine or prepared beef bouillon
1 cup (8 oz. or ½ pt.) sliced fresh or canned mushrooms
1⅓ cups (12-oz. can) tomato paste

4 TO 6 SERVINGS

Cut steak, across grain, into slices ¼ inch thick and about 4 inches long. In fry pan, brown meat in oil. Drain off excess fat; add remaining ingredients. Simmer, covered, 1½ hours until tender. Serve over spaghetti or potatoes.

Tip: To make ahead, prepare and cook; cool and refrigerate or freeze. Reheat, thinning with water, if necessary.

Flank Steak: This long boneless steak comes from the less tender flank area. It is also called London Broil or Plank Steak. It can be very tender and flavorful if simmered with liquid or if tenderized, broiled rare and carved across the long muscle into thin slices for serving.

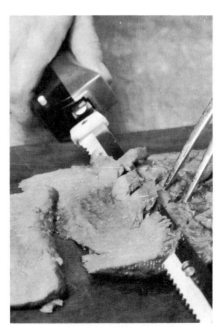

Slicing meat across the grain makes it seem more tender because the fibers are shortened. Tender cuts, as well as less tender cuts, benefit from cross-grain carving. We've sliced our Flank Steak diagonally (across the grain) to shorten the fibers and still leave the slices large enough for attractive serving.

Braised Stuffed Flank Steak, opposite page

This flank steak has a savory stuffing rolled up inside. Cut into slices and serve with sauce in about 2½ hours.

BRAISED STUFFED FLANK STEAK

   1 flank steak (1½ to 2 lbs.)
   2 cups soft bread cubes
   ¼ cup chopped onion or
     1 tablespoon instant minced onion
   ½ cup (1 stalk) chopped celery
   1 tablespoon parsley flakes
   ½ teaspoon powdered sage or thyme
   ½ teaspoon salt
   Dash pepper
   2 tablespoons water or red wine
   2 tablespoons oil or shortening
   1 cup water
   1 beef bouillon cube or
     1 teaspoon instant bouillon

4 TO 5 SERVINGS

Score flank steak on each side at 1-inch intervals. In large mixing bowl, combine bread cubes, onion, celery, parsley, sage, salt, pepper and water; mix well. Place lengthwise down center of meat. Roll up meat with stuffing inside; tie string around roll to hold together. In Dutch oven or fry pan, brown in hot oil. Add water and bouillon cube. Cover and simmer 2 to 2½ hours until tender. Cut across grain into slices and serve with juices.

Tip: If desired, use seasoned dry bread cubes for stuffing; omit sage, salt and pepper, and increase water to 4 tablespoons.

"Cube" Steak: These are less tender pieces of meat that are made tender by mechanical cubing (cutting through the fibers). They are also sold as Minute Steaks.

Economize by using cube steaks in this interesting dish. The sausage in the center and the tasty gravy give the meat a sensational flavor. Round out your meal with baked potatoes, squash and a refreshing salad.

BEEF ROLLETTES

   4 cube steaks (about 1 lb.)
   1 teaspoon salt
   4 smoked sausage links
   2 tablespoons cooking oil
   1¼ cups water
   1 package (⅝ oz.) Pillsbury Home-Style Gravy Mix

4 SERVINGS

Sprinkle meat with salt. Roll sausage link inside each cube steak; secure with toothpicks. Brown in oil in large fry pan. Reduce heat. Combine water and gravy mix; add to steak rolls. Simmer, stirring gently, until mixture thickens and comes to a boil. Continue simmering, covered, 45 to 60 minutes until meat is tender. Serve with sauce.

Tip: To make ahead, prepare, cover and refrigerate. Reheat before serving.

A very special twist to a quick and inexpensive meal. The flavor will remind you of pepper steak, but the preparation time is much shorter. Pictured on page 10

MINUTE STEAK LORRAINE

   2 tablespoons flour
   ½ teaspoon salt
   ⅛ teaspoon minced garlic
   ¼ teaspoon leaf oregano
   6 cube steaks
   2 tablespoons oil or shortening
   1¼ cups water
   ½ cup (4-oz. can) drained mushroom pieces, if desired
   ⅓ cup dry red wine
   1 package (⅝ oz.) Pillsbury Brown Gravy Mix
   ½ green pepper, cut into 1-inch pieces

6 SERVINGS

Combine flour, salt, garlic and oregano. Coat steaks with flour mixture. Brown meat in oil in large fry pan. Reduce heat. Add remaining ingredients. Simmer, covered, for 15 to 25 minutes until steaks are tender and flavors are blended.

A quick 25-minute sauerbraten using cube steaks and gravy mix. A natural with potatoes and sweet sour red cabbage.

MINUTE SAUERBRATEN

   2 tablespoons butter or margarine
   4 beef cube steaks
   Salt
   Pepper
   2 tablespoons chopped onion
   1 cup water
   1 package (⅝ oz.) Pillsbury Brown Gravy Mix
   1 tablespoon brown sugar
   1 tablespoon vinegar

4 SERVINGS

In fry pan, heat butter; add meat and brown on both sides. Season with salt and pepper. Add onion; cook until tender. Stir in water, gravy mix, brown sugar and vinegar. Cook over medium heat, stirring constantly, until mixture boils. Cover and simmer 10 to 15 minutes until meat is tender.

Ground Beef: Meat and trimmings from less tender sections that are ground by mechanical means. There are several different types:

"Hamburger" can contain up to 30% fat. This can include the addition of beef fat above that which is attached to the meat. Because of the large amount of fat, the meat may shrink after cooking.

"Ground beef" contains 20% to 25% fat (only that already on the meat to be ground).

"Ground Chuck" comes from the shoulder (chuck) area and usually includes about 15% to 25% fat.

"Ground round" comes from the round steak area and usually contains less fat than ground chuck. Because it contains less fat, it shrinks less during cooking than ground beef or ground chuck.

"Ground Sirloin" comes from the sirloin steak area and is both the leanest and the highest in price.

Occasionally ground meat is sold in meatloaf mixtures or other such pre-combined foods. If these mixtures include ingredients other than meat, the ingredients will be listed on the label.

Hamburgers — a stand-by for all occasions. Serve them plain or with one of the following variations. They're popular and quick anytime.

HAMBURGERS

 1 lb. ground beef
 1 teaspoon salt
 ⅛ teaspoon pepper
 1 tablespoon Worcestershire sauce
 Dash Tabasco sauce

4 SERVINGS

Combine ground beef with Worcestershire sauce and Tabasco sauce. Shape into patties. In fry pan, fry patties over medium heat 5 to 10 minutes on each side, until browned to desired doneness. If desired, serve with onion slices, mustard and catsup.

Tips: Patties are also good broiled or barbecued over hot coals. Broil 15 minutes for rare and 25 minutes for medium.

The following seasonings can be used for the Worcestershire sauce and Tabasco sauce: 2 to 4 tablespoons chopped onion, 1 tablespoon instant minced onion or 1 tablespoon onion salt. ½ teaspoon garlic salt, ⅛ teaspoon garlic powder or ⅓ teaspoon instant minced garlic. 1 tablespoon Barbecue Sauce. 1 teaspoon prepared mustard and/or 1 tablespoon catsup.

For Cheeseburgers, top each hamburger with 1 slice cheese during last minute of frying. Cover until cheese begins to melt.

Filled hamburgers: Form each patty into two thin patties. Place desired filling between patties; seal edges well.

Filling Suggestions:
Slices of cheese
Chopped canned mushrooms
Mustard
Catsup
Pickle relish
Chopped or sliced pickle

Biscuits cut with doughnut cutter and filled with bean-meat filling mixture. Complete in an hour and a quarter. A delicious way to satisfy hungry appetites!

HUNGRY BOYS' CASSEROLE

 ½ cup (1 stalk) chopped celery
 ¼ cup (½ med.) chopped onion
 ¼ cup chopped green pepper
 1 lb. ground beef
 2 cups (1-lb. can) pork and beans
 ¼ cup catsup
 ¼ cup water
 ½ teaspoon salt
 ½ teaspoon garlic salt

Biscuits

 1 cup Pillsbury All Purpose Flour*
 1½ teaspoons baking powder
 ½ teaspoon salt
 ⅓ cup milk
 3 tablespoons cooking oil
 4 drops yellow food coloring

OVEN 425°   4 TO 5 SERVINGS

Sprinkle celery, onion and green pepper in bottom of 8-inch (1½ qt.) baking dish. Crumble ground beef on top. Bake, uncovered, at 425° for 20 minutes. Remove from oven; drain excess fat. Stir in pork and beans, catsup, water, salt and garlic salt until well blended. Reserve ½ cup of bean-meat mixture. Return casserole to oven for 10 minutes while preparing Biscuits. Arrange Biscuits without centers on casserole. Spoon reserved bean-meat filling in hole of each Biscuit. Top with the biscuit holes. Bake at 425° for 15 to 20 minutes until golden brown.

Biscuits: Combine flour, baking powder and salt in mixing bowl. Combine milk, oil and food coloring. Add to dry ingredients all at once, stirring until dough clings together. Knead on floured surface 8 times. Roll out to ¼-inch thickness. Cut with doughnut cutter, saving holes.

*For use with Pillsbury Self-Rising Flour, omit baking powder and salt.

Have fun with meat loaf — see the Tips for lots of ideas. Dress it up with baked potatoes, a colorful vegetable and relishes or salad.

MEAT LOAF

- 1 lb. ground beef
- ½ cup condensed cream of mushroom soup
- 2 tablespoons dry bread or cracker crumbs
- 1 tablespoon instant minced onion or 1 small onion, chopped
- ¼ teaspoon salt
- ⅛ teaspoon pepper
- 1 teaspoon Worcestershire sauce
- 1 egg

OVEN 350°   ABOUT 4 SERVINGS

In large mixing bowl, combine all ingredients; mix well. Place in greased 8x4-inch (1½ qt.) loaf pan or 8-inch square or round baking pan. Shape into a loaf. Bake at 350° for 40 to 50 minutes. Transfer meat loaf to a platter. If desired, heat remaining soup with 2 tablespoons milk. Serve over meat loaf.

Tips: Try other flavors of cream soups — celery, cheese or tomato.

For a catsup flavor, omit soup; use ¼ cup catsup and increase bread crumbs to ¼ cup.

Meat loaf can also be baked in 4-cup ring mold for 30 to 40 minutes. Turn out of mold and fill center with colorful vegetables or a bowl of mushroom sauce.

For a larger meat loaf, double amounts, using 1 can of soup in meat loaf. Top with catsup or barbecue sauce either before baking or before serving.

Or, form into two separate loaves. Bake one; wrap and freeze the other for a later time. Thaw and bake as directed.

Make individual meat loaves by baking in individual baking cups or muffin cups; fill cups ¾ full. Bake 25 to 30 minutes.

For variety add one of the following to meat mixture:

- 1 cup cubed cheese
- ¼ cup chopped sweet or dill pickle
- 2 tablespoons pickle relish
- ½ cup drained crushed pineapple or pineapple tidbits
- ½ cup drained mushroom pieces
- ¼ cup chopped green pepper

A quick and easy stroganoff made with ground beef and mushroom soup. Serve over rice or noodles, along with buttered carrots and a salad in just 30 minutes.

GROUND BEEF STROGANOFF

- 1 lb. ground beef
- ½ cup (1 small) chopped onion
- ½ cup (4-oz. can) drained mushroom stems and pieces
- 1¼ cups (10½-oz. can) condensed cream of mushroom or celery soup
- ¼ cup water, red wine or beef broth
- ½ cup dairy sour cream or sour half 'n half

4 TO 5 SERVINGS

In fry pan, brown ground beef and onion; drain well. Stir in mushrooms, soup and water. Cover and simmer for 15 to 20 minutes. Stir in sour cream; heat through, but do not boil. Serve over rice, noodles or chow mein noodles.

Tip: For an oven casserole, omit onion and spoon cooked mixture into a 1½ to 2-quart casserole. Top with French fried onions. Bake at 350° for 20 minutes until heated through.

For 2 servings, halve all ingredients. Prepare as directed.

Meatloaf, above, see Tip

PIZZA LOAF

1 package (14.5 oz.) Pillsbury Refrigerated Seasoned Pizza Dough and Pizza Sauce
1 lb. ground beef
¼ cup chopped onion or 1 tablespoon instant minced onion
½ cup (4-oz. can) drained mushroom stems and pieces
2 tablespoons flour
1 teaspoon paprika
¼ teaspoon leaf oregano
⅛ teaspoon pepper
½ cup chopped black olives, if desired
1 cup (4 oz.) shredded Cheddar cheese
Milk
Sesame seeds

Sauce

1⅓ cups (10¾-oz. can) condensed tomato soup
1 cup (4 oz.) shredded Cheddar cheese
½ teaspoon dry mustard
1 teaspoon Worcestershire sauce

OVEN 400°   6 TO 8 SERVINGS

In fry pan, brown ground beef, drain well. Add refrigerated pizza sauce, onion, mushrooms, flour, paprika, oregano and pepper to meat. Cook over medium heat 15 minutes. Remove from heat and stir in olives. Cool for 10 minutes.

Open can of pizza dough; unroll and place seasoned side up on a greased cookie sheet. Stretch dough to a 14x11-inch rectangle.

Place meat mixture down center third of dough to within 2-inches of ends. Sprinkle with Cheddar cheese. Make diagonal cuts 2-inches apart, on each side of rectangle just to edge of filling. Fold ends over filling. Then fold strips over filling, alternating sides and crossing in center. Brush with milk and sprinkle with sesame seeds. Bake at 400° for 15 to 20 minutes until golden brown. Serve as is or with Sauce.

Sauce: Combine tomato soup, shredded cheese, dry mustard and Worcestershire sauce in a saucepan. Heat over low heat until cheese is melted and mixture is smooth. Serve hot.

Tip: Reheat in foil at 350° for 20 to 25 minutes until heated through.

1. Place meat mixture down center third of dough.
2. Make diagonal cuts 2-inches apart on each side.
3. Fold strips over filling, crossing in center.
4. Sprinkle with sesame seeds.

EASY STROGANOFF

1 lb. ground beef
⅓ cup chopped onion
2 tablespoons flour
1⅓ cups (10¾-oz. can) condensed vegetable soup
½ cup (4-oz. can) drained mushroom stems and pieces
2 tablespoons parsley flakes
1 teaspoon Worcestershire sauce
½ teaspoon garlic salt
½ teaspoon salt
⅛ teaspoon pepper
¾ cup dairy sour cream

6 TO 8 SERVINGS

In large fry pan, brown ground beef; drain excess fat. Add onion; cook until onion is tender. Stir in remaining ingredients except sour cream. Simmer, covered, for 15 to 20 minutes until flavors are blended. Stir in sour cream. Continue simmering until heated through, but do not boil. Serve over noodles.

BEEF 'N BEAN SUPPER DISH

1 lb. ground beef
½ cup (1 med.) sliced onion
½ teaspoon salt
¼ teaspoon pepper
3¼ cups (1 lb. 12-oz. can) pork and beans
½ cup catsup
½ tablespoon Worcestershire sauce
2 tablespoons brown sugar
1 tablespoon vinegar
¼ teaspoon Tabasco sauce

4 TO 6 SERVINGS

In large fry pan, brown ground beef and onion; drain excess fat. Add remaining ingredients; mix well. Simmer, covered, 20 to 30 minutes until flavors are well blended. Serve hot.

Tips: If desired, Beef 'N Bean Supper Dish can be served as a sandwich on buns.

For 2 to 3 servings, halve all ingredients. Prepare as directed.

Beef 'n Bean Supper Dish, opposite page

There are treasures within treasures in these sealed and seeded rounds of biscuits. Ready, gang, in about an hour!

HIDDEN SURPRISE BURGERS

1 lb. ground beef
½ cup dry bread crumbs or soda cracker crumbs
¼ cup catsup
1 teaspoon salt
1 teaspoon Worcestershire sauce
½ teaspoon onion salt
5 (1½ x ¼ in.) pieces of cheese
1 can (9.5 oz.) Pillsbury Refrigerated Hungry Jack Flaky or Flaky Buttermilk Biscuits
Milk
Poppy seeds or sesame seeds

OVEN 375°   5 SERVINGS

Combine ground beef, bread crumbs, catsup, salt, Worcestershire sauce and onion salt in mixing bowl. Divide into 10 equal portions. Flatten each to a 4-inch circle on waxed paper or plastic wrap. Place a piece of cheese in center of 5 patties. Place remaining 5 patties on top of cheese. Pinch edges together well to seal in cheese. Smooth edges to make 4-inch patties. Open can of biscuits; separate dough into 10 biscuits. On ungreased cookie sheet, pat 5 of the biscuits to make 5-inch circles. Place a patty on top of each; moisten edges with milk. Press out remaining biscuits to 5-inch circles. Stretch over patty and seal to bottom crust. Pinch together well to seal. Brush with milk and sprinkle with poppy seeds or sesame seeds. Bake at 375° for 25 to 30 minutes. Remove from cookie sheet immediately. Allow to cool 10 minutes before eating.

Tips: Patties can be made ahead, covered and refrigerated, until ready to place inside biscuits and bake.

Use any of your favorite fillings for the cheese.

A twist on tacos, this fun-to-eat ground beef dish will be a favorite with your family. Serve it with a salad and refried beans. OLE!

TICO TACOS

1 lb. ground beef
½ cup (1 med.) chopped onion or 2 tablespoons instant minced onion
½ cup (4 oz.) shredded Cheddar cheese
1 medium tomato, chopped
½ teaspoon salt
Few drops Tabasco sauce or taco sauce
2 cans (8 oz. each) Pillsbury Refrigerated Buttermilk or Country Style Biscuits
1 cup shredded lettuce (about ⅛ medium head)
¼ cup chopped ripe olives

Cheese Sauce

1 cup (8-oz. jar) pasteurized process cheese spread
Few drops Tabasco sauce or taco sauce

OVEN 400°   30 SNACKS OR 10 MAIN DISH SERVINGS

In large fry pan, brown ground beef; drain excess fat. Add onion, cheese, tomato and seasonings. Mix well. Separate biscuit dough into 20 biscuits. Roll out or press 10 biscuits into 5-inch circles on ungreased cookie sheets. Spoon about ⅓ cup meat mixture on each circle. Roll out or press remaining 10 biscuits into 5-inch circles. Place over filling. Seal edges with fork. Bake at 400° for 12 to 15 minutes until golden brown. Serve at once, topped with shredded lettuce, Cheese Sauce and chopped olives.

Cheese Sauce: Combine ingredients and heat over medium low heat, stirring constantly.

Tip: For added flavor, ¼ teaspoon chili powder can be added to meat mixture.

So Mexican with a mildly spiced enchilada dish. Beans and a salad go well with this easy dish.

EASY ENCHILADA BAKE

1 to 1¼ lbs. ground beef
1 clove garlic, minced or ⅛ teaspoon instant minced garlic
1 to 1⅓ cups chopped onion
¾ cup water
½ cup barbecue sauce
½ to 1 tablespoon chili powder
½ teaspoon salt
2 cups (8 oz.) shredded Cheddar cheese
Reserved chopped onion

Tortillas

Cornmeal
1 can (8 oz.) Pillsbury Refrigerated Buttermilk or Country Style Biscuits

OVEN 350°   4 TO 5 SERVINGS

In large fry pan, brown ground beef; drain. Stir in ⅓ cup of onion (reserve remaining onion for filling), water, barbecue sauce, chili powder and salt. Simmer 5 minutes. While sauce simmers, prepare Tortillas. Place 1 tablespoon cheese and 1 tablespoon onion down center of each Tortilla. Roll each Tortilla and place seam-side down in ungreased 12x8-inch (shallow 2 qt.) or 9-inch square baking dish. Cover with warm meat mixture. Sprinkle on any remaining cheese and onion. Bake at 350° for 25 to 30 minutes until cheese has melted and center is no longer doughy.

Tortillas: Sprinkle cornmeal on work surface. Separate biscuit dough into 10 biscuits. Coat both sides of biscuits with cornmeal; roll or pat out to 5-inch circles.

Tips: Reheat, covered with foil, at 350° for 15 to 20 minutes until heated through.

To make ahead, prepare, cover and refrigerate up to 2 hours before baking. Bake as directed.

If desired, prepared Tortillas can be used.

Easy Enchilada Bake, opposite page

43

crackers and garnish with crushed corn chips, if desired.

Tip: To make ahead, prepare, cool, cover and refrigerate or freeze. Reheat, adding additional water, if necessary.

SAUCY CRESCENT RAVIOLI

    1 to 1¼ lbs. ground beef
    1⅔ to 2 cups (about 15 oz.)
        spaghetti sauce with meat*
    1 tablespoon instant minced
        onion or ¼ cup chopped
        onion
    1 tablespoon flour
    1 teaspoon parsley flakes
    ¼ teaspoon garlic salt
    1 can (8 oz.) Pillsbury
        Refrigerated Quick
        Crescent Dinner Rolls
    3 slices American cheese,
        cut into quarters or 1 cup
        (4 oz.) shredded Cheddar
        cheese

OVEN 375°   4 TO 6 SERVINGS

In large fry pan, brown ground beef; drain. Stir in ½ cup spaghetti sauce (reserve remaining sauce for topping), onion, flour and parsley flakes. Set aside. Separate crescent dough into 4 rectangles. Firmly press perforations to seal (this prevents separation during baking). Place 3 tablespoons of meat filling along one long side of each rectangle. Fold dough over filling, pressing edges to seal. Cut each folded rectangle into 3 squares. Spread remaining meat filling in bottom of ungreased 12x8-inch (shallow 2 qt.) or 9-inch square baking dish. Place squares over meat filling. Bake at 375° for 15 minutes. Remove from oven. Place a cheese quarter on each square; pour on remaining spaghetti sauce. Bake 10 to 15 minutes more until cheese has melted and sauce is bubbly.

Tips: *One package spaghetti sauce mix can be used for canned sauce. Prepare according to package directions and use as directed.

Reheat, covered with foil, at 375° for 15 to 20 minutes until heated through.

To make ahead, prepare, cover and refrigerate up to 2 hours before baking. Bake as directed.

BEEF'N WIENER BAR-B-QUE

    1 lb. ground beef
    ½ lb. wieners, sliced ¼-inch
        thick
    ¼ cup barbecue sauce
    ¾ cup water
    1 tablespoon sugar, if
        desired
    2 tablespoons dry onion
        soup mix*

                    4 TO 6 SERVINGS

In medium fry pan, brown ground beef; drain. Add remaining ingredients. Cover and simmer 15 to 20 minutes; serve over toasted hamburger buns.

Tip: *If desired, use 1 tablespoon instant minced onion and 1 beef bouillon cube for onion soup.

EASY CHILI

    1 lb. ground beef
    1 medium onion, sliced
    ½ cup (1 med.) chopped
        green pepper
    2 cups (1-lb. can) undrained
        tomatoes
    2 cups (1-lb. can) undrained
        red kidney beans
    1 cup (8-oz. can) tomato
        sauce
    1 teaspoon salt
    2 to 2½ teaspoons chili
        powder
    1½ teaspoons prepared or dry
        mustard
    1 clove garlic or ⅛ teaspoon
        garlic powder

                    4 TO 6 SERVINGS

In large fry pan or saucepan, brown ground beef; drain off excess fat. Add remaining ingredients. Simmer, uncovered, for 1 hour, stirring occasionally. Remove garlic clove before serving. Serve with assorted

LAYERED MEAT LOAF

    1½ lbs. ground beef
    1½ teaspoons salt
    ⅛ teaspoon pepper
    1 egg
    ½ cup dry bread or cracker
        crumbs
    ½ cup milk

Dressing

    2 cups soft bread cubes
    ½ cup (½ stalk) chopped
        celery
    1 tablespoon instant minced
        onion or ¼ cup chopped
        onion
    1 tablespoon minced parsley
    1 tablespoon water
    1 teaspoon salt
    ⅛ teaspoon pepper
    1 egg

OVEN 350°   6 SERVINGS

Combine all ingredients except Dressing; blend well. Prepare Dressing. Press half of meat mixture in 9x5-inch (2 qt.) loaf pan. Top with Dressing and then remaining half of meat, pressing to form loaf. Bake at 350° for 50 to 60 minutes. Let stand 5 minutes; loosen edges and turn out of pan. Spoon catsup or barbecue sauce over top.

Dressing: in mixing bowl, combine all ingredients.

Tip: If desired, prepare meat loaf a few hours ahead and refrigerate. Bake as directed.

Easy Chili, opposite page

SWEDISH MEAT BALLS

> 1 lb. ground beef
> ¼ cup finely chopped onion or 1 teaspoon instant minced onion
> 3 tablespoons dry bread crumbs or cracker crumbs
> 1 teaspoon salt
> ⅛ teaspoon pepper
> ⅛ to ¼ teaspoon ground nutmeg
> 1 egg
> 1 tablespoon oil or shortening
> 2 tablespoons flour
> 1 cup water
> 1 beef bouillon cube or 1 teaspoon instant beef bouillon

4 SERVINGS

In mixing bowl, combine ground beef, onion, bread crumbs, salt, pepper, nutmeg and egg. Mix until well blended. Shape into 1-inch balls. In fry pan, brown on all sides in hot oil. Remove meat balls. Stir flour into drippings; cook over low heat until flour browns. Add water and bouillon cube. Cook, stirring constantly, until mixture comes to a boil. Reduce heat; add meat balls. Cover and simmer for 15 to 20 minutes. Serve over rice or mashed potatoes.

Tips: For an easy mushroom sauce, brown meat balls and drain off drippings. Add 1¼ cups (10½-oz. can) condensed golden mushroom soup and ¼ cup water. Cover and simmer 20 minutes.

If desired, add ¼ cup dry sherry for part of water.

To make ahead, cook, cool and refrigerate or freeze. Reheat, adding additional water if necessary.

For 2 servings, prepare meatballs as directed, shaping into balls. Freeze half of uncooked meatballs for later use. Prepare remaining meatballs as directed, using

2 teaspoons oil or shortening, 1 tablespoon flour, ½ cup water and ½ beef bouillon cube.

MEATBALL DINNER

> 1 medium onion, sliced
> ½ lb. ground beef
> 1 egg
> ¼ cup dry bread crumbs or soda cracker crumbs
> 2 tablespoons milk
> ½ teaspoon salt
> ¼ teaspoon leaf basil
> Dash pepper
> 1⅓ cups (10¾-oz. can) condensed tomato soup
> 2 cups (1-lb. can) undrained mixed vegetables*
> 1 teaspoon Worcestershire sauce

OVEN 425°   4 TO 5 SERVINGS

Arrange onion slices on bottom of 8-inch square (1½-qt.) baking dish. Combine ground beef, egg, bread crumbs, milk, salt, basil and pepper. Shape into 1-inch meatballs. Place on top of onion slices. Bake at 425° for 20 minutes. Remove from oven; drain excess fat. Add tomato soup, mixed vegetables and Worcestershire sauce. Stir just to blend. If desired, sprinkle with Parmesan cheese. Continue baking for 30 to 35 minutes.

Tips: *If desired, 1½ cups (10-oz. pkg.) frozen mixed vegetables can be used for the canned; add ½ cup water. Other vegetables can be used for the mixed vegetables, using 1 cup vegetables and ⅔ cup liquid or water.

To make ahead, prepare meat mixture. Cover and store in refrigerator. Bake as directed.

SWEET 'N SOUR MEATBALLS

> 1 lb. ground beef
> ¼ cup dry bread or cracker crumbs
> 2 tablespoons finely chopped onion or ½ teaspoon instant minced onion
> ½ teaspoon salt
> ⅛ teaspoon pepper
> 1 tablespoon oil or shortening
> ¼ cup sugar
> 2 tablespoons cornstarch
> 2 tablespoons soy sauce
> 2 tablespoons vinegar
> ½ cup water
> ½ cup reserved pineapple syrup
> 1½ to 2 green peppers, cut into 1-inch pieces
> 1¼ cups (13¼-oz. can) drained pineapple tidbits or chunks (reserve syrup)

4 TO 5 SERVINGS

In large mixing bowl, combine ground beef, bread crumbs, onion, salt and pepper; mix well. Shape into 1-inch balls. Brown in hot oil in fry pan. Drain off drippings; remove meatballs. Combine sugar and cornstarch in fry pan; stir in soy sauce, vinegar, water and pineapple syrup. Cook, stirring constantly, until mixture boils and thickens. Add green pepper, pineapple and meatballs. Cover and simmer 15 to 20 minutes. Serve over rice.

Tip: To make ahead, prepare, cool and refrigerate or freeze. To serve, reheat, adding additional water if necessary.

CRAFTY CRESCENT LASAGNE

- 2 slices (7x4 in.) Mozzarella cheese
- 1 tablespoon milk
- 1 tablespoon sesame seeds

Meat Filling

- ½ lb. sausage
- ½ lb. ground beef
- ¾ cup chopped onion or 3 tablespoons instant minced onion
- ½ clove garlic, minced
- 1 tablespoon parsley flakes
- ½ teaspoon leaf basil
- ½ teaspoon leaf oregano
- ½ teaspoon salt
- Dash pepper
- ¾ cup (6-oz. can) tomato paste

Cheese Filling

- 1 cup creamed cottage cheese
- 1 egg
- ¼ cup grated Parmesan cheese

Crust

- 2 cans (8 oz. each) Pillsbury Refrigerated Quick Crescent Dinner Rolls

OVEN 375°   4 TO 6 SERVINGS

Spread half of Meat Filling lengthwise down center half of Crust to within 1 inch of each 13-inch end. Top Meat Filling with Cheese Filling; spoon remaining Meat Filling over top, forming 3 layers. Place cheese slices over Meat Filling. Fold 13-inch ends of dough rectangle over 1 inch of filling. Pull long sides of dough rectangle over filling, being careful to overlap edges only ¼ inch. Pinch overlapped edges to seal. Brush with milk; sprinkle with sesame seeds.

Bake at 375° for 20 to 25 minutes until deep golden brown.

Meat Filling: In large fry pan, brown meat; drain excess fat. Add onion, garlic, parsley, seasonings and tomato paste. Simmer, uncovered, for 5 minutes. (Meat mixture can be made ahead and refrigerated.)

Cheese Filling: Combine all ingredients.

Crust: Unroll crescent dough and separate into 8 rectangles. On ungreased cookie sheet, place dough rectangles together overlapping edges (about a 15x13-inch rectangle). Press edges and perforations to seal. (This prevents leaking during baking.)

Tip: Lasagne can be prepared ahead of time, covered with plastic wrap, and refrigerated for 2 to 3 hours before baking. Increase baking time to 25 to 30 minutes.

Crafty Crescent Lasagne, above

POPPIN' FRESH BARBECUPS

¾ lb. ground beef
½ cup barbecue sauce
1 tablespoon instant minced onion
2 tablespoons brown sugar
1 can (8 oz.) Pillsbury Refrigerated Flaky Tenderflake or Tenderburst Baking Powder Biscuits
¾ cup shredded Cheddar or American cheese

OVEN 400°   10 OR 12 BARBECUPS

In large fry pan, brown ground beef; drain. Add barbecue sauce, onion and brown sugar. Set aside. Separate biscuit dough into biscuits. Place each biscuit in an ungreased muffin cup, pressing dough up sides to edge of cup. Spoon meat mixture into cups. Bake at 400° for 10 to 15 minutes until golden brown. Sprinkle with cheese; return to oven to melt cheese.

Tip: To make ahead, cool meat mixture thoroughly. Spoon into cups; cover and refrigerate up to 2 hours. Bake as directed.

Poppin' Fresh Barbecups, above

STACK-A-ROLL STROGANOFF

1 lb. ground beef
½ cup (4-oz. can) drained mushroom stems and pieces
2½ cups (3½-oz. can) French fried onions, reserve ½ cup for garnish
1⅓ cups (10½-oz. can) condensed cream of mushroom soup
½ cup dairy sour cream
1 can (9.5 oz.) Pillsbury Refrigerated Hungry Jack Flaky or Buttermilk Flaky Biscuits
Reserved ½ cup French fried onions

Topping:

½ cup dairy sour cream
1 egg
1 teaspoon celery seed
½ teaspoon salt

OVEN 375°   6 SERVINGS

Brown ground beef; drain well. In an ungreased deep casserole (2½ or 3 qt.), combine ground beef, mushrooms and French fried onions; toss lightly. In saucepan, bring undiluted mushroom soup to a boil; stir in ½ cup sour cream. Separate biscuit dough into 10 biscuits. Cut each biscuit in half crosswise forming 20 half circles. Pour warm soup mixture evenly over meat; immediately arrange biscuits, cut-side down, in a circle around edge of casserole. Sprinkle reserved onions between biscuits. Pour Topping over biscuits. Bake at 375° for 25 to 30 minutes until golden brown.

Topping: In small mixing bowl, combine all ingredients; blend well.

Tips: If desired, 1⅓ cups (10½-oz. can) cream of celery soup can be used for cream of mushroom soup.

If desired, use 2 to 3 cups cubed, cooked beef for ground beef; omit browning.

Reheat, loosely covered, at 375° for 10 to 15 minutes.

MEXICALI MEATLOAF

1 egg
1 lb. lean ground beef
¾ cup (7-oz. can) drained whole kernel corn with sweet peppers
½ cup soda cracker crumbs
½ cup chili sauce
2 tablespoons sweet pepper flakes, if desired
1 tablespoon instant minced onion
½ teaspoon leaf oregano
4 sliced stuffed green olives, if desired
6 slices crisp, crumbled bacon, if desired

Topping:

1 egg, slightly beaten
2 tablespoons milk
½ teaspoon salt
½ teaspoon dry mustard
½ teaspoon Worcestershire sauce
1 cup (4 oz.) shredded Cheddar cheese

OVEN 425°   6 SERVINGS

Beat egg slightly in mixing bowl. Add ground beef, corn, cracker crumbs, chili sauce, sweet pepper flakes, onion and oregano. Mix well. Press meat mixture firmly into 9x5-inch loaf pan. Bake at 425° for 20 to 25 minutes. Spread Topping on meatloaf. Top with olives and bacon. Bake an additional 5 minutes or until cheese melts. Let stand 10 minutes before serving.

Topping: Combine egg and milk; add salt, dry mustard, Worcestershire sauce and cheese.

MEATBALLS IN GINGER SAUCE

    1 lb. ground beef
    1 egg
    2 cups (2 slices) soft bread
      cubes
    ¼ cup water
    1 tablespoon instant minced
      onion or ¼ cup chopped
      onion
    1 teaspoon salt
    ¼ teaspoon pepper
    1 tablespoon cooking oil
    1½ cups water
    2 cubes beef bouillon or
      2 teaspoons instant beef
      bouillon
    ⅓ cup brown sugar
    ¼ cup dark seedless raisins,
      if desired
    2½ tablespoons lemon juice
    ½ cup coarse gingersnap
      crumbs

4 TO 5 SERVINGS

In large mixing bowl, combine ground beef, egg, bread cubes, ¼ cup water, onion, salt and pepper; mix well. Shape into 25 1½-inch balls. Brown meatballs in oil in large fry pan. Remove meatballs from fry pan. In same fry pan, combine remaining ingredients. Simmer, stirring constantly, until mixture thickens and comes to a boil. Add meatballs to sauce. Simmer, covered, for 20 to 30 minutes until meatballs are cooked through.

Tip: To serve as hors d'oeuvres, shape into ½ to 1-inch balls. Cook as directed. Serve with toothpicks for easy eating.

To make ahead, brown meatballs and prepare sauce. Refrigerate or freeze. When ready to serve, continue cooking as directed.

STEWING MEAT

Stew Meat: Lean squares of meat which are cut from the less tender sections and require long, slow simmering.

A western beef stew that's hearty enough for a cowboy! Beans and a tomato-flavored sauce give it a simply grand flavor! See the Tip for a chili variation.
Pictured on page 51

HEARTY BEEF AND BEAN STEW

    1½ to 2 lbs. beef stew meat
    2 tablespoons oil or
      shortening
    2 cups (two 8-oz. cans)
      tomato sauce
    1 cup water
    2 teaspoons salt
    ¼ teaspoon pepper
    ⅛ teaspoon ground thyme
    1 bay leaf
    1 package (⅝ oz.) Pillsbury
      Brown Gravy Mix
    6 carrots, cut into 2-inch
      pieces
    1 cup (2 stalks) sliced celery
    1¾ cups (15-oz. can) undrained
      kidney beans
    1 cup (8-oz. can) undrained
      small whole onions or
      2 tablespoons instant
      minced onion

6 TO 8 SERVINGS

In large fry pan or Dutch oven, brown meat in oil. Reduce heat. Add tomato sauce, water, salt, pepper, thyme and bay leaf. Simmer, covered, for 1½ hours. Add remaining ingredients. Continue simmering, stirring occasionally, for ½ hour until carrots are tender. Serve hot.

Tip: For Hearty Chili, add 1 tablespoon ground chili powder to mixture with tomato sauce.

Serve this over noodles or see Tip for making a hearty soup. Add a vegetable and molded fruit salad to complete your meal.

HUNGARIAN GOULASH

    2 lbs. boneless beef, cut into
      1½-inch cubes
    ¼ cup flour
    2 tablespoons oil or
      shortening
    2 large or 3 medium onions,
      sliced
    ½ cup (1 med.) chopped
      green pepper
    1 clove garlic, minced or ⅛
      teaspoon instant minced
      garlic
    1 to 2 tablespoons paprika
    2 teaspoons salt
    1 teaspoon caraway seeds, if
      desired
    ½ teaspoon ground marjoram
      or 1 teaspoon leaf
      marjoram, if desired
    ¼ teaspoon pepper
    2 cups (1-lb. can) undrained
      canned tomatoes
    1½ cups water
    3 tablespoons flour
    ½ cup water

6 TO 8 SERVINGS

Coat beef cubes with ¼ cup flour. In Dutch oven, brown beef and onions in hot oil. Add green pepper, garlic, paprika, salt, caraway seeds, marjoram, pepper, tomatoes and 1½ cups water. Simmer, covered, for 2 hours until meat is tender. Combine 3 tablespoons flour with ½ cup water. Blend into meat mixture. Bring to boil, stirring constantly. Serve over noodles or potatoes.

Tips: To make ahead, prepare and cook except for thickening; cool and refrigerate or freeze. To serve, reheat and thicken with flour mixture.

For a hearty Hungarian Soup, cut beef into bite-size pieces and use 2½ cups water.

BEEF STEW WITH DUMPLINGS

2 lbs. stewing beef, cut into
  1-inch cubes
¼ cup flour
1 tablespoon salt
¼ teaspoon pepper
2 tablespoons cooking oil
4 cups water
2 onions, sliced
1 bay leaf
6 carrots, cut into 1-inch
  strips
6 potatoes, cut into quarters,
  if desired
1 teaspoon Kitchen bouquet,
  if desired
1½ cups (10-oz. pkg.) frozen
  peas

Dumplings

1½ cups Pillsbury All Purpose
  Flour*
2 teaspoons baking powder
½ teaspoon salt
½ cup currants, if desired
1 egg, slightly beaten
½ cup milk
2 tablespoons cooking oil
1 teaspoon instant minced
  onion

8 TO 10 SERVINGS

Combine flour, salt and pepper. Coat meat with flour mixture. Brown meat in oil in a Dutch oven or large fry pan. Stir in water, sliced onions, bay leaf, salt and pepper. Cover; simmer for 1½ to 2 hours until meat is tender. Remove bay leaf. Add carrots, potatoes and Kitchen bouquet. Cover and cook 20 to 30 minutes until almost tender. Add peas. Drop 8 to 10 tablespoons of Dumpling mixture on top of stew. Cover. Steam 12 to 15 minutes until dumplings are done in center. Do not remove cover during steaming.

Dumplings: Combine flour, baking powder, salt and currants in mixing bowl. Add egg, milk, oil and onion. Mix only until moist.

*For use with Pillsbury Self-Rising Flour, omit baking powder and salt.

BEEF RAGOUT

2 lbs. beef stew meat
¼ cup flour
2 teaspoons salt
¼ teaspoon pepper
2 medium onions, sliced
2 tablespoons cooking oil
1 cup water
1 cup Burgundy, red wine
  or water
½ cup (4-oz. can) undrained
  mushroom pieces
1 beef bouillon cube or
  1 teaspoon instant bouillon
1 stick cinnamon, if desired
1 bay leaf
1 cup (2 stalks) chopped
  celery
1 cup (2 med.) sliced carrots

6 TO 8 SERVINGS

Combine flour, salt and pepper. Coat meat pieces with flour mixture. Brown meat and onion slices in oil in large fry pan or Dutch oven. Reduce heat; add water, Burgundy, mushrooms, bouillon, cinnamon and bay leaf. Simmer, covered, for 1½ hours. (For milder cinnamon flavor, remove cinnamon stick after ½ to 1 hour.) Add carrots and celery. Continue simmering ½ hour until meat and carrots are tender. Remove cinnamon stick and bay leaf; serve over rice, noodles or potatoes.

BEEF STEW

1½ to 2 lbs. boneless beef, cut
  into 1½-inch cubes
¼ cup flour
2 teaspoons salt
¼ teaspoon pepper
3 tablespoons oil or
  shortening
1 stalk celery, cut into pieces
2 medium onions, quartered
1 bay leaf
4 cups water
4 potatoes, cut into quarters
6 carrots, cut into pieces
1 cup (½ pt.) whole fresh
  mushrooms, if desired
2 tablespoons flour
¼ cup water

5 TO 6 SERVINGS

Coat meat with mixture of ¼ cup flour, salt and pepper. Brown in hot oil in Dutch oven or large fry pan. Add celery, onions, bay leaf and water. Cover; simmer for 1½ hours until tender. Remove bay leaf. Add potatoes, carrots and mushrooms. Cover; continue cooking until vegetables are tender 30 to 45 minutes. To thicken liquid, combine 2 tablespoons flour with ¼ cup water. Add to cooking liquid. Cook until mixture boils and thickens.

Tips: If desired, use ½ to 1 cup red wine for part of water; or 1 cup (8-oz. can) tomato sauce for part of water.

Add other favorite vegetables, too: cabbage, rutabagas, peas, beans, etc.

To make ahead, cook meat, cool and refrigerate or freeze. One hour before serving, (if frozen, thaw first), add vegetables and continue as directed.

Stew is good topped with favorite dumplings about 20 minutes after vegetables have been added. Cook as directed in dumpling recipe.

For 2 to 3 servings, halve all ingredients. Prepare as directed.

Beef Ragout

Hearty Beef and Bean Stew, page 49

51

Onion soup adds a tasty, easy flavor to short ribs. Serve in 2¼ hours with noodles, broccoli and a fruit salad; or start meat the night before (see Tip) for a quick meal.

SAVORY ONION SHORT RIBS

3 tablespoons flour
½ cup (1 envelope) dry onion soup mix
3 lbs. beef short ribs, cut into serving pieces
2 tablespoons oil or shortening
1½ cups water
½ cup chopped green pepper
1 teaspoon salt

5 TO 6 SERVINGS

Combine flour and soup mix; roll meat in mixture. (Reserve remaining mixture.) Brown meat in hot oil in fry pan. Pour off drippings. Add 1 cup of the water, green pepper and salt. Simmer 2 hours until tender. Remove meat to heated platter. Skim off fat. Blend reserved flour mixture with remaining ½ cup of the water. Stir into drippings until well blended and smooth. Bring to a boil. Pour over ribs and serve.

Tip: To make ahead, prepare except for thickening juices; cool and refrigerate or freeze. Reheat and thicken juices.

Oven barbecued short ribs that take no watching — just start baking 1¾ hours before serving. For a complete oven meal, serve with baked potatoes and foil-wrapped corn on the cob, plus a relish tray or crisp green salad.

BARBECUED SHORT RIBS

3 to 3½ lbs. beef short ribs, cut into serving pieces
1 cup catsup
½ cup water
½ cup (1 med.) chopped onion
¼ cup firmly packed brown sugar
3 tablespoons Worcestershire sauce
2 teaspoons garlic salt
1 teaspoon salt
2 teaspoons prepared mustard
¼ teaspoon powdered thyme
1 lemon, sliced

OVEN 350°   4 TO 6 SERVINGS

Place ribs in baking dish or casserole. Combine remaining ingredients; pour over ribs. Cover and bake at 350° for 1½ to 2 hours until tender. Skim off fat and serve with sauce.

Tips: For a quick barbecue sauce, combine 1 cup of your favorite prepared barbecue sauce with the water, onion and lemon. Pour over meat and continue as directed.

To make ahead, refrigerate ribs in sauce either before or after cooking. Bake as directed or reheat to serve.

The cooked ribs also freeze well.

A hearty meal-in-one for a cool fall evening. Complete your meal with warm bread and a crisp salad.

Add any of your favorite vegetables or leftover vegetables — canned, frozen or fresh — to this hearty soup. Serve generous portions of soup with French or Italian bread.

This hearty soup is a winner on chilly day suppers. Chock-full of vegetables and beef, it goes perfectly with a salad and hot bread.

OLD FASHIONED VEGETABLE SOUP

2½ lbs. beef shank or meaty soup bone
1 tablespoon (3 tsp.) salt
⅛ teaspoon ground thyme
6 peppercorns
1 bay leaf
2 whole allspice
2 beef bouillon cubes
6 cups hot water
2 cups (2 med.) cubed raw potato
2 medium stalks celery, sliced
2 medium carrots, sliced
½ cup (1 small) chopped onion or 2 tablespoons instant minced onion
2 cups (1-lb. can) undrained tomatoes
1½ cups (12-oz. can) drained whole kernel corn

6 TO 8 SERVINGS

In large saucepan (5 qt.), combine beef shank, salt, thyme, peppercorns, bay leaf, allspice, bouillon cubes and hot water. Simmer, covered, about 3 hours until meat is tender. Remove beef shank, peppercorns and bay leaf; cut meat from bone into chunks and return to soup. Add remaining ingredients. Continue simmering, covered, about 30 minutes until vegetables are tender.

Tips: Any combination of vegetables can be used in the soup. If desired, add cubed parsnips or turnips, chopped green pepper, chopped cabbage, green beans or lima beans.

Soup can be prepared in a pressure cooker according to manufacturer's directions.

To make ahead, prepare broth, removing meat from bone. Cover and freeze up to 3 weeks. Add vegetables to thawed broth and prepare as directed.

OXTAIL STEW

2 lbs. oxtails
2 tablespoons flour
2 tablespoons oil or shortening
¾ cup (1 large) chopped onion
1 bay leaf
2 teaspoons salt
¼ teaspoon pepper
1 tablespoon vinegar
2 cups water
2 to 3 medium potatoes, cut into pieces
3 carrots, cut into pieces
2 stalks celery, cut into pieces
1 green pepper, cut into pieces

4 TO 6 SERVINGS

Coat oxtails with flour. In Dutch oven or deep fry pan, brown oxtails in hot oil. Add onion and brown slightly. Add bay leaf, salt, pepper, vinegar and water. Simmer 2 to 2½ hours until tender. Remove bay leaf. Add vegetables; simmer 30 to 45 minutes until tender. If desired, thicken juices with 2 tablespoons flour mixed with ¼ cup water. Bring to a boil.

Tips: If desired, omit vinegar and use 1 cup water and 1 cup dry red wine instead of the 2 cups water.

To make ahead, prepare and cook except for adding vegetables. Cool and refrigerate or freeze. Reheat, add vegetables and continue as directed.

MINESTRONE SOUP

2 to 3 lbs. beef shank
4 quarts (16 cups) water
1 tablespoon (3 tsp.) salt
2 cups chopped cabbage
2 cups (1-lb. 4-oz.) can) undrained chick peas or kidney beans
2 cups (1-lb. can) undrained tomatoes
2 cups (4 med.) sliced carrots
1½ cups (10-oz. pkg.) frozen peas
1 cup (2 stalks) sliced celery
1 cup (¼ lb. or 4 oz.) spaghetti, broken into 2 to 3-inch pieces
1 bay leaf
1 to 2 tablespoons salt
½ teaspoon pepper

4 QUARTS

Combine beef shanks, water and salt in large (5 qt.) saucepan or Dutch oven. Bring to a boil; simmer, covered, for 2½ to 3 hours until meat is tender. Remove beef shank from soup. Separate meat from bone; return meat to soup. Add remaining ingredients. Continue simmering 30 to 45 minutes until vegetables are tender. Remove bay leaf. If desired, garnish with parsley sprigs before serving.

Tip: To make ahead, prepare broth as directed, removing meat from bone and returning to broth. Refrigerate or freeze until ready to use. Proceed as directed.

Come For Fondue

Fondue is a fun meal for company! Everyone gets into the action as each person cooks his own food. Several types of fondue pots (including electric, with thermo-statically controlled heat) are available in a variety of colors and styles. A metal pot or one with a non-stick or enamel lining is best for beef fondue. Ceramic pots may crack from the high temperatures needed to heat the oil.

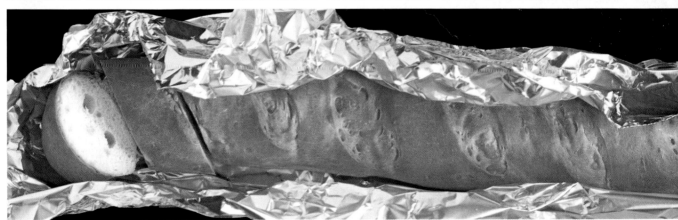

French or Italian breads (or other such munching foods) go very well with fondue. Try serving the bread sliced, warmed and buttered with garlic or herb butter; or, serve it whole and let each person break off his own.

Long handled, two-pronged forks are great for dipping the meat and transfering it to the plate. Sectioned plates are specially designed for a variety of sauces.

Rosé, claret or burgundy wines are good choices to serve with this dish. Coffee or tea can be served with dessert.

Fondue makes a fun meal for company. Each guest cooks his own meat in the hot oil; then eats with one of the sauces. Serve with lots of hot French bread, a vegetable casserole and a pretty tossed salad.

BEEF FONDUE

2 lbs. boneless sirloin or tenderloin, cut into 1-inch cubes
Sauces
Cooking oil

4 SERVINGS

Arrange cubes of meat in individual dishes lined with lettuce leaves; place at each place setting. Set out 3 to 4 sauces. (Try bottled steak sauces, horseradish sauce, cocktail dips, mustard sauce, teriyaki sauce, bleu cheese salad dressing or make your own sauces — see recipes that follow.) Place fondue pot in center of table. Heat cooking oil until about 375° or until it browns a cube of bread quickly. Place oil in fondue pot over heating unit.

Each guest uses fondue fork to spear meat and then cooks in hot oil until of desired doneness. Remove to plate and eat with dinner fork (the fondue fork becomes very hot in the oil), dipping into desired sauces. For an added treat, pass a bowl of chopped salted peanuts along with the sauces.

Tips: Try other types of fondue — use cubes of lamb (serve with chutney, sweet and sour and curry sauces) or fresh or frozen shrimp, thawed and well drained, (serve with cocktail, sweet and sour or curry sauces).

If you want to have vegetables with fondue, add whole fresh mushrooms or cubes of raw eggplant to dishes of meat. Each guest cooks vegetable along with meat.

If oil becomes too cool, place on range for a few minutes to reheat.

You can strain the leftover oil and store in refrigerator; use the next time you serve fondue.

GARLIC BUTTER

½ cup butter or margarine, softened
1 clove garlic, minced, or ⅛ teaspoon instant minced garlic or garlic powder or ½ teaspoon garlic salt

Cream butter until very creamy. Blend in garlic; leave at room temperature until served.

CHIVE BUTTER

½ cup butter or margarine, softened
3 tablespoons chopped chives
2 tablespoons chopped parsley
¼ teaspoon salt
Dash cayenne pepper, if desired

Cream butter until very creamy; blend in remaining ingredients, mixing well. Leave at room temperature until served.

BUTTERY STEAK SAUCE

6 tablespoons butter or margarine, softened
¼ teaspoon salt
½ teaspoon dry mustard, if desired
2 teaspoons lemon juice
1 teaspoon Worcestershire sauce
Dash pepper

Cream butter until very creamy; blend in remaining ingredients, mixing well. Leave at room temperature until served.

HOT CATSUP SAUCE

½ cup catsup
½ tablespoon vinegar
½ teaspoon horseradish
Dash Tabasco sauce

Combine all ingredients; mix well. Refrigerate until served.

CURRY SAUCE

½ cup dairy sour cream
½ teaspoon curry powder
⅛ teaspoon salt
Dash Tabasco sauce

Combine all ingredients; mix well. Refrigerate until served.

Pork

Pork and ham (cured pork) rank second to beef in popularity in the United States.

Thought to be the first mammal domesticated for food, pork and ham were also very important in the early American diet. Because of its adaptability to environment, it traveled West along with the settlers. And today, the majority of pork in the United States comes from the Midwest. Some is marketed as fresh pork; other is cured and/or smoked.

Pork is a tender meat. Although it doesn't require the long, slow cooking for tenderizing, it does require thorough cooking. Cuts of pork can be barbecued or broiled if they are cooked at a moderate temperature that allows the meat to cook thoroughly without drying the surface. Some cuts — bacon, ham and chops — are cured and smoked before selling to give them a special flavor.

High quality pork should have a grayish pink color and a relatively firm and fine grained flesh that is free from excessive moisture. The lean tissue should be moderately marbled and covered with a layer of firm, white fat. Pork is most plentiful from October through January.

Braised Pork Chops, Page 61

PORK ROASTS

Pork Loin Roast: A roast from the loin or rib section. It is sometimes boned and tied and sold as a roll. Rib sections from two loins are sometimes tied together to form a Crown Roast. Loin and rib chops are also cut from this section. The loin is sometimes cured and smoked — for roasts or chops.

Shoulder Roasts: These include: Arm Roast (cut from the arm section of the shoulder and identified by the round arm bone), Fresh Boston Shoulder (contains the blade bone exposed on two surfaces and is sometimes called Boston Butt), and Boneless Rolled Roast. These make tender roasts, but unless boned, they contain bone and more fat than a Loin Roast.

Serve this delicious pork roast with oven baked potatoes, green beans and a salad of sliced tomatoes.

PORK LOIN ROAST

4 to 5 lbs. center-cut pork
   loin roast
Salt
Pepper

OVEN 325°   8 SERVINGS

Have meat man remove backbone from loin. Place roast, fat side up, on a rack in an open shallow roasting pan. Season with salt and pepper. Insert meat thermometer so the bulb reaches the center thickest part, being sure that the bulb does not rest in fat or on bone. (Do not add water; do not cover.) Roast at 325° for 30 to 35 minutes per lb. until thermometer registers 170°.

How To Carve

Have meat man saw backbone free from ribs for easier carving. Saw cut should not cut into meaty center.

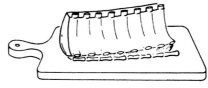

Before the roast is brought to the table, remove the backbone. Do this by cutting close along the bone, leaving as much meat on roast as possible. Place roast with bone side facing carver.

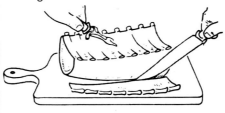

Insert the fork in the top of the roast. Make slices by cutting close along each side of the rib bone. One slice will contain the rib, the next will be boneless.

A delicious and colorful roast for fall or winter dinners. Start roast 4 hours ahead; then serve with baked squash, broccoli and tossed salad.
Pictured on page 8

CRANBERRY-STUFFED PORK CROWN ROAST

7 lbs. pork crown roast
1½ teaspoons salt
¼ teaspoon pepper

Cranberry Stuffing:

4 cups dry bread cubes
1½ cups chopped cranberries
¼ cup sugar
2 tablespoons finely chopped onion or 2 teaspoons instant minced onion
2 tablespoons grated orange peel
1 teaspoon salt
½ teaspoon leaf marjoram or ⅛ teaspoon powdered marjoram
¼ teaspoon leaf thyme or Dash powdered thyme
½ cup butter or margarine, melted
½ cup orange juice

OVEN 325°   6 TO 8 SERVINGS

For easy carving, have meat man cut off backbone. Season meat with salt and pepper. Place in roasting pan, rib bones up. Wrap tips of bones in foil to prevent excess browning. Insert meat thermometer so the bulb reaches center of thickest part but does not rest in fat or on bone. (Do not add water; do not cover.) Roast at 325° for 2 hours. Meanwhile prepare Cranberry Stuffing. Fill center with stuffing and roast 1½ to 2 hours longer, until meat is well done and meat thermometer registers 170°. To serve, remove foil and cover bone ends with paper frills or spiced crabapples.

Cranberry Stuffing: Combine all ingredients; toss lightly.

Tip: If desired, use seasoned bread cubes for stuffing, omitting salt, marjoram and thyme.

Pork Loin Roast, opposite page, with Oven Baked Carrots

Pork Tenderloin: The lean muscle that runs along the back; this is considered the most tender cut of pork.

A tasty, crunchy sesame seed stuffing bakes between two split pork tenderloins. Start preparing 2¼ hours ahead.

SESAME-STUFFED TENDERLOINS

2 pork tenderloins
¼ cup sesame seeds
¼ cup chopped celery
2 tablespoons chopped onion or 2 teaspoons instant minced onion
¼ cup butter or margarine
2 cups dry bread cubes
1 teaspoon salt
½ teaspoon poultry seasoning or powdered thyme
⅛ teaspoon pepper
1 teaspoon Worcestershire sauce
1 egg, slightly beaten
1 tablespoon lemon juice

OVEN 325°   6 SERVINGS

Cut each tenderloin almost through lengthwise; flatten. Sauté sesame seeds, celery and onion in butter in fry pan until lightly browned. Add remaining ingredients. Toss lightly. Spread stuffing on cut surface of 1 tenderloin. Place remaining tenderloin, cut-side down, on stuffing; fasten with string or skewers. Place on rack in open roasting pan. Roast at 325° for 1½ to 2 hours until well done.

Tip: If desired, use seasoned bread stuffing cubes, omitting salt, poultry seasoning and pepper.

TIMETABLE FOR ROASTING PORK ROASTS
OVEN 325°

CUT	Weight	Meat Thermometer Reading	Approx. Cooking Time per Lb.
Loin			
Center	3-5 lbs.	170°	30-35 min.
Half	5-7 lbs.	170°	35-40 min.
End	3-4 lbs.	170°	40-45 min.
Roll	3-5 lbs.	170°	35-45 min.
Boneless			
Top	2-4 lbs.	170°	30-35 min.
Crown	4-6 lbs.	170°	35-40 min.
Picnic			
Shoulder (fresh)			
Bone-In	5-8 lbs.	185°	30-35 min.
Rolled	3-5 lbs.	170°	35-40 min.
Boston Shoulder	4-6 lbs.	185°	45-50 min.
Leg (fresh ham)			
Whole (bone-in)	10-14 lbs.	185°	30-35 min.
Whole (rolled	7-10 lbs.	170°	30-35 min.
Half (bone-in)	5-7 lbs.	170°	35-40 min.
Tenderloin	½-1 lb.		45-60 min.

A marinade lends a subtle flavor to this delicious and tender roast. Have your meat man remove backbone from loin roast before you start.

PROVENCE-STYLE PORK ROAST

4 to 6 lbs. pork loin roast
2 cloves garlic, slivered
2 teaspoons salt
¼ teaspoon pepper
1 cup dry white wine
2 tablespoons parsley flakes or chopped parsley

OVEN 325°   8 TO 10 SERVINGS

Make small cuts between ribs and insert garlic slivers. Sprinkle roast with salt and pepper. In large plastic bag or large shallow pan, pour wine over roast; rub on parsley. Cover; marinate, turning occasionally, 2 to 4 hours. Drain wine. Place roast, fat-side up, on a rack in an open shallow roasting pan. Insert meat thermometer so the bulb reaches the center of thickest part, being sure that the bulb does not rest in fat or on bone. (Do not add water; do not cover.) Roast at 325° for 30 to 35 minutes per lb. until thermometer registers 170°.

CHOPS AND STEAKS:

Loin Chops: These chops have two muscles (one on each side of the T-shaped bone) and are cut from the loin area. They are also sometimes cured and smoked and are sold as Smoked Pork Chops.

Rib Chops: These have only one muscle and come from the rib area. They are sometimes cut extra thick and a cut made into the rib side for stuffing. These chops are occasionally cured and smoked and are sold as Smoked Pork Chops.

Shoulder Steaks: These steaks are from the shoulder area so they contain several small muscles. They are sometimes referred to as Arm Chops or Steaks (identified by the round arm bone) or Blade Chops or Steaks (identified by the blade bone).

Smoked pork chops add interest to a family or company meal. Try serving them breaded along with spinach or cooked cabbage and a fruit salad.

Try broiling smoked pork chops with one of these brush-on glazes. They're ready to serve in 15 minutes.

To vary flavor, try different fruit or vegetable juices — orange, pineapple, tomato. Add color to your meal with a vegetable and crispness with a salad.
Pictured on page 4, 56

BREADED SMOKED PORK CHOPS

- ⅓ cup dry bread crumbs
- ¼ teaspoon powdered thyme or 1 teaspoon leaf thyme
- ½ cup coarsely crushed French fried onion rings, if desired
- ¼ cup chopped cashews, if desired
- 1 egg, slightly beaten
- 4 smoked pork chops

OVEN 350°   4 SERVINGS

Combine bread crumbs, thyme, onion rings and cashews. Dip each chop into egg and then coat with crumb mixture. Place in shallow baking dish. Bake at 350° for 30 to 35 minutes until golden brown.

Tip: If desired, prepare chops several hours ahead, cover and refrigerate. Bake just before serving.

HONEY SMOKED CHOPS

- 4 smoked pork chops
- ¼ to ½ cup honey or marmalade

4 SERVINGS

Place chops on broiler pan; broil for 5 minutes. Brush with honey; broil 5 minutes. Turn; brush with remaining honey and broil 5 more minutes.

Tips: For variety, brush chops with honey celery seed dressing in place of honey.

For 2 servings, halve all ingredients. Prepare as directed.

BRAISED PORK CHOPS

- 6 rib, loin or shoulder pork chops, cut ¾ to 1-inch thick
- ½ teaspoon salt
- ⅛ teaspoon pepper
- ¼ cup water, fruit juice or vegetable juice

6 SERVINGS

Brown chops on both sides in large fry pan. Season with salt and pepper; add water. Cover; simmer 45 to 60 minutes until tender.

Tip: For 3 servings, halve all ingredients. Prepare as directed.

"Frenched" chops or rib roasts have had the meat and fat removed from the last 1 inch of the rib bone. The bone ends can be decorated by placing paper frills over the bones after cooking.

Orange Stuffed Pork Chops, opposite page

This orange and raisin stuffing is a perfect compliment for pork chops. Serve with mashed potatoes, green vegetable and a crisp salad.

ORANGE STUFFED PORK CHOPS

    4 loin or rib pork chops, cut
        1½ to 2-inches thick
    2 cups soft bread cubes
    2 tablespoons raisins
    2 tablespoons chopped onion
        or 1 teaspoon instant
        minced onion
    ¼ teaspoon salt
    ¼ teaspoon poultry seasoning
    3 tablespoons orange juice

OVEN 325°   4 SERVINGS

Cut a deep slit or pocket in pork chops, cutting almost to the bone. In large mixing bowl, combine bread cubes, raisins, onion, salt, poultry seasoning and orange juice; mix well. Place stuffing in slit in each chop. (If you have extra stuffing, place on top of chops just before baking.) Tie chop together with string or secure with toothpicks. Place in baking dish. Sprinkle with salt and pepper. Cover and bake at 325° for 1¼ to 1½ hours until tender.

Tips: Two thin pork chops can be used for each thick pork chop. Sandwich stuffing between each; secure edges together. Bake as directed.

If desired, use 2 cups seasoned bread stuffing cubes for soft bread cubes; omit salt and poultry seasoning.

Breaded pork chops are always a favorite. Serve in 1 hour with spinach, warm rolls and coleslaw.

BREADED PORK CHOPS

    6 rib or loin pork chops, cut
        ¾ to 1-inch thick
    1 egg, slightly beaten
    ½ cup dry bread or cracker
        crumbs
    1 teaspoon salt
    ¼ teaspoon pepper
    3 tablespoons oil or
        shortening
    ⅓ cup water
    ½ teaspoon Worcestershire
        sauce

                              6 SERVINGS

Dip pork chops into egg, then into mixture of bread crumbs, salt and pepper. Brown in hot oil on both sides in large fry pan. Add water and Worcestershire sauce. Cover and simmer 45 to 60 minutes, until tender. Uncover and brown chops on both sides until crisp, about 10 minutes.

Tip: For 2 to 3 servings, halve all ingredients, except egg. Prepare as directed.

Two favorites — combined into one dish. Add a green vegetable and a molded salad for a complete meal.

PORK CHOPS WITH SCALLOPED POTATOES

    6 pork chops, cut ¾ -inch
        thick
    1 tablespoon oil or
        shortening
    1 package (5⅛ oz.) Pillsbury
        Scalloped Potato Mix
    2 tablespoons catsup
    ½ teaspoon salt
    ⅛ teaspoon pepper
    Dash Tabasco sauce

OVEN 350°   6 SERVINGS

Brown pork chops on both sides in oil in fry pan. Prepare potatoes as directed on package, adding catsup and seasonings with the milk. Arrange potatoes in a 2-quart shallow baking dish or fry pan. Bake at 350° for 30 minutes. Place chops on potatoes and bake 45 minutes longer.

Cheese-flavored puffs top these baked pork chops. Complete your menu with corn, a green vegetable and a molded salad.

CHEESE PUFF PORK CHOPS

    4 pork chops
    ½ teaspoon salt
    1 tablespoon cooking oil

Cheese Topping

    ½ cup Pillsbury All Purpose
        Flour*
    2 tablespoons cooking oil
    ½ teaspoon baking powder
    ⅔ cup milk
    2 eggs
    ⅓ cup grated Parmesan
        cheese or Cheddar cheese
    2 tablespoons instant minced
        onion
    ½ teaspoon salt
    ¼ teaspoon pepper
    Paprika, if desired

OVEN 350°   4 SERVINGS

In large fry pan, brown pork chops on both sides. Sprinkle with salt. Place chops in 9-inch (2 qt.) baking dish. Spread with Cheese Topping to cover completely. Sprinkle lightly with paprika. Bake uncovered at 350° for 50 to 60 minutes until lightly brown on top.

Cheese Topping: In medium saucepan, blend in flour, oil and baking powder. Gradually add milk. Cook over medium heat, stirring constantly until very thick. Remove from heat and blend in unbeaten eggs, one at a time. Add Parmesan cheese, onion, salt and pepper. Blend thoroughly.

Tip: If the fry pan used for browning can be placed in the oven, there's no need to change meat to baking dish. Cook it all right in the fry pan.

*For use with Pillsbury Self-Rising Flour, omit baking powder and salt.

Stuffing baked on top of the chops saves time and adds convenience to this dish. For the pork chop lovers in your family! Coleslaw, spiced apples and a green vegetable complete the menu.

BAKED PORK CHOPS AND STUFFING

- 4 pork chops
- 1 tablespoon oil
- 2 cups (2 slices) soft bread cubes
- 2 tablespoons chopped onion or 2 teaspoons instant minced onion
- ¼ cup melted butter or margarine
- 2 tablespoons water
- ¼ teaspoon poultry seasoning
- 1¼ cups (10½-oz. can) condensed cream of mushroom soup
- ⅓ cup water

OVEN 350°   4 SERVINGS

In large fry pan, brown pork chops in oil. Place chops in shallow baking dish (2 to 2½ qt.) Lightly mix together bread, onion, butter, 2 tablespoons water and poultry seasoning. Place mound of stuffing on top of each chop. Blend soup and ⅓ cup water; pour over chops. Bake, uncovered, at 350° for 1 hour until meat is tender. If desired, garnish with parsley or pimiento.

Try pork chops with a snappy barbecue sauce. Serve in an hour with peas and carrots and rolls.

BARBECUED PORK CHOPS

- 4 shoulder pork chops or pork steaks
- 1 cup barbecue sauce
- ½ cup water
- ½ cup (1 med.) chopped onion or 2 tablespoons instant minced onion
- ½ teaspoon salt
- ⅛ teaspoon pepper
- 1 clove garlic, minced or ⅛ teaspoon instant minced garlic

4 SERVINGS

In large fry pan, brown chops on both sides. Drain off fat. Combine remaining ingredients; pour over chops. Simmer for 30 minutes; turn and simmer for 15 more minutes. Skim off fat; serve sauce over chops.

Tip: To make your own barbecue sauce, combine ½ cup catsup, ¼ cup vinegar, 2 tablespoons brown sugar and 1 teaspoon Worcestershire sauce with the salt, pepper, onion, garlic and water.
For 2 servings, halve all ingredients. Prepare as directed.

If you like sweet 'n sour pork, you'll love these pork chops. Serve with rice and sliced tomatoes in 1¼ hours.

SWEET 'N SOUR PORK CHOPS

- 6 rib, loin or shoulder pork chops, cut ¾ to 1-inch thick
- 1 bouillon cube or 1 teaspoon instant bouillon
- 1 cup water
- ¼ cup vinegar
- ¼ cup sugar
- ¼ cup chopped onion or 1 tablespoon instant minced onion
- ¾ cup (8¼-oz. can) undrained pineapple chunks
- 2 tablespoons soy sauce
- ½ green pepper, cut into rings
- 2 tablespoons cornstarch
- 2 tablespoons water

6 SERVINGS

In large fry pan, brown chops on both sides. Add bouillon cube, water, vinegar, sugar, onion, pineapple, soy sauce and green pepper. Cover and simmer 1 hour. Combine cornstarch and 2 tablespoons water. Remove chops to heated platter. Stir cornstarch mixture into cooking liquid. Cook, stirring constantly, until mixture is thickened and clear. Serve over chops.

Pork chops dressed up with a flavorful sour cream sauce go perfectly with rice or noodles. Add a green vegetable and an apple salad to complete your meal in less than 1 hour.

PORK CHOPS IN SOUR CREAM SAUCE

- 4 shoulder, rib or loin pork chops or pork steaks
- 1½ teaspoons instant minced onion or 2 tablespoons chopped onion
- ⅛ teaspoon instant minced garlic or 1 clove garlic, minced
- ½ cup water
- ¼ cup catsup or chili sauce
- 2 tablespoons brown sugar
- 1 bouillon cube or 1 teaspoon instant bouillon
- 2 tablespoons flour
- ¼ cup water
- ½ cup dairy sour cream

4 SERVINGS

In fry pan, brown chops on both sides. Add onion, garlic, ½ cup water, catsup, brown sugar and bouillon. Cover and simmer 30 to 40 minutes until tender. Combine flour with ¼ cup water. Remove chops to heated platter; add flour mixture to cooking liquid. Cook, stirring constantly, until mixture boils and thickens. Reduce heat; add sour cream. Heat, but do not boil. Serve over meat along with noodles or rice.

Tips: To make ahead, prepare except for thickening with flour. Cool and refrigerate or freeze. To serve, reheat and continue as directed.

For special occasions, use pork tenderloin in place of pork chops; cut into 2-inch pieces and flatten into fillets. One whole pork tenderloin will make about 4 servings.

Try this for your next party or special family meal — pork in a sweet and tangy sauce over rice. Party time in about 45 minutes.

Party Pork Barbecue

PARTY PORK BARBECUE

  1 lb. pork shoulder, cut into 1-inch cubes
  ¼ cup flour
1½ teaspoons salt
  ⅛ teaspoon pepper
  2 tablespoons oil or shortening
  1 cup (2 stalks) sliced celery
  1 medium green pepper, cut into 2-inch strips
  1 small onion, sliced
1½ cups (13¼-oz. can) undrained pineapple tidbits or chunks
  ¾ cup catsup
  1 tablespoon prepared mustard
  1 tablespoon Worcestershire sauce

5 to 6 SERVINGS

Coat pork with mixture of flour, salt and pepper. Brown in oil in large fry pan, adding any remaining flour. Add celery, green pepper, onion, pineapple, catsup, mustard and Worcestershire sauce. Simmer, covered, 30 minutes. Serve over rice.

Tips: To keep warm, put rice in ovenproof dish or casserole, pushing rice up around edges. Pour barbecue-pork mixture in center. Place in warm oven for up to 30 minutes.

This recipe can be prepared ahead and refrigerated or frozen. Then, reheat to serve.

For 2 to 3 servings, halve all ingredients. Prepare as directed.

PORK AND LIMA HOTDISH

1½ lbs. pork shoulder, cut into cubes
1 teaspoon salt
¼ teaspoon pepper
1 tablespoon cooking oil
1½ cups (1-lb. 1-oz. can) drained small lima beans
1 cup (8½-oz. can) drained small onions
1 cup (8-oz. can) undrained tomatoes, cut into pieces
Grated Cheddar or American cheese, if desired

OVEN 350°   4 TO 5 SERVINGS

Sprinkle meat with salt and pepper. Brown in oil large fry pan. In ungreased 2 to 2½-quart casserole or baking dish, spread beans and onions over bottom. Place browned meat cubes on top of onions; top with tomato pieces. Sprinkle grated cheese over top. Bake, covered, at 350° for 1 to 1½ hours until meat is tender. Serve over rice.

CREOLE PORK STEAKS

4 to 6 pork steaks (1 to 1½ lbs.)
1 tablespoon cooking oil
½ cup (1 stalk) sliced celery
2 cups (two 8-oz. cans) tomato sauce
1½ cups water
2 tablespoons brown sugar
1 teaspoon salt
¼ to ½ teaspoon leaf basil
1 cup uncooked regular rice

4 TO 6 SERVINGS

In large fry pan, brown steaks in oil. Remove steaks; brown celery

in same fry pan. Drain excess oil. Add remaining ingredients; stir to combine. Add steaks. Bring mixture to a boil. Reduce heat; simmer, covered, 30 minutes until rice is cooked.

Tip: Pork chops can be used for the pork steaks. Prepare as directed.

POLYNESIAN PORK

1 lb. lean boneless pork, cut into 1-inch cubes
2 tablespoons flour
1 tablespoon oil or shortening
½ teaspoon salt
½ cup water
2 green peppers, cut into 1-inch pieces
1½ cups (13¼-oz. can) undrained pineapple tidbits or chunks
¼ cup sugar
¼ cup vinegar
2 tablespoons cornstarch
2 tablespoons soy sauce
1 medium or 2 small tomatoes, cut into 8 pieces

4 SERVINGS

Coat pork cubes with flour. Brown in hot oil on all sides in large fry pan. Add salt and water; simmer, covered, 30 minutes. Add green pepper, pineapple, sugar and vinegar. Combine cornstarch and soy sauce. Stir into meat mixture. Bring to a boil, stirring constantly; cover and simmer 10 minutes. Add tomatoes and simmer 5 minutes, stirring occasionally. Serve over rice or chow mein noodles.

Tip: For 2 servings, halve all ingredients. Prepare as directed.

CHOW MEIN

1 lb. chow mein meat
1 tablespoon oil or shortening
1 cup (8 oz. or ½ pt.) sliced fresh mushrooms
1 medium onion, sliced
1 cup (2 stalks) sliced celery
½ teaspoon salt
½ teaspoon ground ginger
3 tablespoons soy sauce
1 bouillon cube or 1 teaspoon instant bouillon
1 cup water
2 cups (1-lb. can) drained bean sprouts
⅔ cup (5-oz. can) sliced, drained water chestnuts
½ cup (5-oz. can) drained bamboo shoots
1 tablespoon cornstarch
2 tablespoons water

4 SERVINGS

In fry pan, brown meat in hot oil. Add mushrooms and onion; brown slightly. Add celery, salt, ginger, soy sauce, bouillon and 1 cup water. Cover and simmer 20 minutes. Add bean sprouts, water chestnuts and bamboo shoots. Combine cornstarch with 2 tablespoons water. Stir into meat mixture; bring to boil, stirring constantly. Cover and simmer 15 more minutes. Serve over chow mein noodles or rice.

Tips: Two cups (1-lb. can) drained chow mein vegetables can be used for bean sprouts, water chestnuts and bamboo shoots.

For crisper vegetables, add onion and celery along with bean sprouts.

If desired, use 1 package (⅝ oz.) Pillsbury Brown Gravy Mix for salt, bouillon cube and cornstarch.

Cubes of pork make a flavorful and quick stew since it doesn't need long simmering. Top with dumplings and serve with a salad in about an hour.

DUBLIN STEW WITH DUMPLINGS

 1 lb. pork shoulder, cut into 1-inch cubes
 ⅓ cup flour
 2 tablespoons oil or shortening
 ½ cup (1 med.) chopped onion
 4 carrots, cut into pieces
 ½ cup (1 stalk) chopped celery
 1 clove garlic, minced or ⅛ teaspoon instant minced garlic
 2 cups water
 1½ teaspoons salt
 3 beef bouillon cubes or 3 teaspoons instant beef bouillon
 1½ cups (10-oz. pkg.) frozen mixed vegetables or frozen peas

DUMPLINGS

 1 cup Pillsbury All Purpose Flour*
 2 teaspoons sugar
 1½ teaspoons baking powder
 ½ teaspoon salt
 ¼ teaspoon dry mustard
 ¼ teaspoon caraway seed, if desired
 ⅓ cup milk
 2 tablespoons cooking oil
 1 egg

6 SERVINGS

Coat pork shoulder with flour. Brown in oil in Dutch oven; add onion and remaining flour; brown slightly. Add carrots, celery, garlic, water, salt and bouillon. Cover and simmer for 30 minutes. (Meanwhile prepare Dumplings.) Stir in mixed vegetables; bring mixture to boil again. Drop Dumplings by tablespoon onto hot stew; cover and simmer for 15 minutes until Dumplings are done in center. (Do not remove cover while cooking.)

Dumplings: Combine flour with sugar, baking powder, salt, mustard and caraway seed in mixing bowl. Combine milk, oil and egg. Add to flour mixture all at once, stirring only until moistened.

*For use with Pillsbury Self-Rising Flour, omit baking powder and salt.

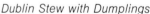

Dublin Stew with Dumplings

This rich and flavorful soup will delight the hearty eaters of your family. An economizing dish that's good for you, too.

PORK AND LENTIL SOUP

1½ lbs. pork shanks
  2 cups (1-lb. pkg.) lentils
10 to 12 cups water
  1 tablespoon (3 tsp.) salt
  1 tablespoon Worcestershire sauce
  6 peppercorns or
  ¼ teaspoon pepper
  1 onion, sliced or
  2 tablespoons instant minced onion
  1 cup (2 stalks) sliced celery
  1 cup (2 med.) sliced carrots

8 TO 10 SERVINGS

In large saucepan (5 qt.) or Dutch oven, combine all ingredients, except celery and carrots. Simmer, covered, 2 hours until meat is tender. Remove peppercorns and pork shanks. Cut meat from bone and fat; return meat to soup. Add celery and carrots. Continue simmering ½ hour until vegetables are tender.

Tips: To make ahead, prepare soup and remove meat from bone. Cover and freeze up to 3 weeks or refrigerate for about a week. Add celery and carrots to thawed soup and continue as directed.

A hearty, meaty soup that can be made ahead or made in your pressure cooker for convenience.

HAM & SPLIT PEA SOUP

2 cups (16-oz. pkg.) split peas
2 lbs. ham shank
½ cup (small) chopped onion or 2 tablespoons instant minced onion
½ teaspoon salt
½ teaspoon sweet basil
6 peppercorns
8 cups water
2 medium stalks celery, sliced
1 medium carrot, chopped, if desired

6 TO 8 SERVINGS

In large saucepan (5 qt.), combine all ingredients except celery and carrots. Simmer, covered 2 to 2½ hours until peas are tender and soup thickens. Add celery and carrots. Continue simmering about 30 minutes until vegetables are tender. Remove peppercorns and ham shank; cut meat from bone into chunks and return to soup. If desired, top servings with crumbled bacon, paprika or sieved hard-cooked egg.

Tip: To make ahead, prepare broth, removing meat from bone. Cover and freeze up to 3 weeks or refrigerate for about a week. Add remaining ingredients to thawed broth and prepare as directed.

Homemade soups need little attention. They cook by themselves and leave you free.

For extra quick homemade soup, follow the tips and use a pressure cooker.

Most soups freeze well so they are an easy Sunday night supper to pull from the freezer.

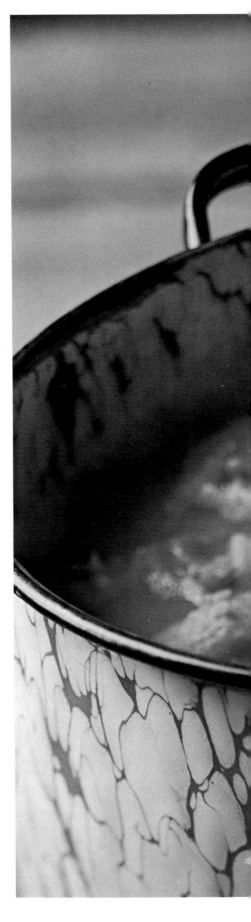

Ham & Split Pea Soup, opposite page

Start these easy baked ribs 2¼ hours ahead. Serve with rice, green beans and a molded fruit salad.

BARBECUED SPANISH RIBS

4 lbs. spareribs or country-style ribs, cut into serving pieces
1 tablespoon (3 tsp.) salt
1 teaspoon paprika
1 teaspoon chili powder
¼ teaspoon pepper
¼ teaspoon cayenne pepper, if desired
2 tablespoons vinegar
¾ cup catsup
¾ cup water
2 medium onions, sliced

OVEN 325°   6 TO 8 SERVINGS

Place meat in shallow baking dish. Combine remaining ingredients except onion. Pour over ribs. Top with onion slices. Bake at 325° for 1 hour. Turn ribs; continue baking 1 hour longer. Baste ribs occasionally with sauce while baking. Skim off fat and serve sauce over ribs.

The orange and soy flavors add a sweet-sour touch to these spareribs. Serve over rice in 2¼ hours.

POLYNESIAN SPARERIBS

3 to 3½ lbs. spareribs, cut into 3-rib pieces
1 teaspoon salt
¼ teaspoon pepper
1 cup water
⅓ cup firmly packed brown sugar
2 tablespoons cornstarch
½ teaspoon ground ginger
2 tablespoons soy sauce
½ cup vinegar
1 to 2 cloves garlic, minced or ⅛ to ¼ teaspoon instant minced garlic
2 oranges, sliced

6 SERVINGS

In large fry pan, brown meat on both sides. Sprinkle with salt and pepper. Add water. Cover and simmer 1 hour. Remove meat; skim off excess fat. In small bowl, combine brown sugar, cornstarch, ginger, soy sauce, vinegar and garlic. Add to liquid in pan. Cook, stirring constantly, until thickened and clear. Add ribs and spoon sauce over to coat. Arrange orange slices on top. Cover. Simmer, covered, 1 more hour, adding water if necessary. Serve with rice.

Tips: Country-style ribs can also be used.

To make ahead, prepare sauce and add precooked spareribs. Cool and refrigerate or freeze. Simmer or bake, covered, for 1 hour, adding water if necessary.

When using a thermostatically controlled surface unit, use flat bottom utensils so that a good contact between utensil and sensing device is maintained.

Serve this family favorite with potatoes and sliced tomatoes. Start 1¾ hours ahead or prepare part the night before. See Tip.

BAKED SPARERIBS AND SAUERKRAUT

3 lbs. spareribs, cut into 3 rib pieces
4 cups (1-lb. 12-oz. can or 1 qt.) undrained sauerkraut
2 tart apples, peeled and chopped
¼ cup (1 small) chopped onion
¼ cup water
2 tablespoons brown sugar

OVEN 350°   5 TO 6 SERVINGS

In large fry pan, brown ribs; drain off fat. Salt and pepper to taste. In 13x9-inch (3 qt.) baking dish, combine sauerkraut, apples, onion, water and brown sugar. Place ribs on top; bake uncovered at 350° for 1½ hours until ribs are tender, stirring occasionally.

Tips: Country-style ribs can be used for spareribs; cut into serving pieces.

To make ahead, cover ribs with salted water; cover and simmer for 1 hour. Drain and combine with remaining ingredients in baking dish. Cool and refrigerate. Bake uncovered at 350° for 45 to 60 minutes, stirring occasionally.

For 2 to 3 servings, halve all ingredients. Prepare as directed, baking for 1¼ to 1½ hours.

Baked Spareribs and Sauerkraut, opposite page

71

Curing was originally used as a way to preserve meat. Today the distinctive flavor it produces is still popular. Curing (done by treating meat with a brine mixture) changes the flavor and produces the typical red color. Meats are frequently smoked after curing by using special woods, such as hickory or maple.

HAM CUTS: Hams are available fully-cooked (need no further cooking) and cook-before-eating (partially cooked in processing but need further cooking).

Smoked Ham: Ham cuts have the characteristic single round bone. Hams are from the back leg of pork and have been cured and smoked. They are available as bone-in, semi-boneless, boneless and shaped or rolled. In addition, they can be sold whole, halved, or as pieces. The shank half is the lower half (extending down the leg); the butt half is the upper half.

Rolled or Shaped Hams: These cuts have been boned, rolled or shaped, and are sometimes in a casing. They are fully cooked, and no further cooking is necessary. However, heating contributes to the flavor, and slices can easily be baked, broiled or fried.

Semi-boneless Hams: Trimmed hams with all bones except the leg bone removed. These are usually available in a casing or wrapped in paper; most are fully cooked.

Canned Hams: These are cured hams (some are smoked, too) that have been trimmed and boned and are fully-cooked. They have almost no waste from fat or bone.

Ground Ham: Meat and trimmings from less tender sections that are ground mechanically.

How To Carve

Place the ham on the platter with the shank to the carver's right. Remove several slices from the thin side to form a solid base on which to set the roast.

Turn the roast on its base. Starting at the shank end, a small wedge cut is removed; then carve perpendicular to the leg bone as shown.

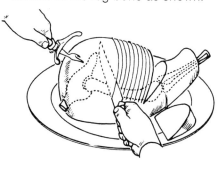

Release slices by cutting under them and along the leg bone, starting at the shank end. For additional servings, turn over to the original position and make slices to the bone, release and serve.

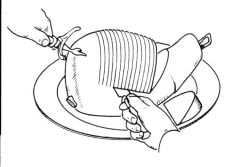

Choose a cook-before-eating, a fully cooked or a canned ham; then, bake it to perfection topped with a shiny glaze. Allow ½ to ¾ lb. of ham per serving.

Pictured on page 79

BAKED SMOKED HAM

1 smoked ham

OVEN 325°

Place ham, fat-side up, on rack in open shallow roasting pan. Insert meat thermometer so the bulb reaches the center of the thickest part, but does not rest in fat or on bone. (Do not add water; do not cover.) Bake at 325° as directed below. To glaze baked ham, pour off drippings from pan. If necessary, trim off fat, leaving just a thin layer on ham. Score ham by cutting diamond shapes about ¼-inch deep through the fat. If desired, insert a whole clove in each diamond. Spoon one of the suggested glazes over ham; return to oven and bake 15 to 20 more minutes.

Glazes (enough for whole ham):

Brown Sugar: Combine 1 cup firmly packed brown sugar, 2 tablespoons flour, ½ teaspoon dry or 1 teaspoon prepared mustard, ⅛ teaspoon cinnamon and 3 tablespoons dry sherry, vinegar or water; mix well. Spread over ham.

Jelly: Heat 1 cup currant or apple jelly until melted. Spread over ham.

Orange Marmalade: Use 1 cup orange marmalade to spread over ham.

Pineapple: Combine 1 cup firmly packed brown sugar with ¾ cup drained crushed pineapple; spread over ham.

Start with a simple ham loaf, then vary with a special topping or shape. Serve with green beans and baked potatoes in 1¼ hours.

HAM LOAF

- 1½ lbs. ground smoked ham
- ½ cup soft bread cubes
- 2 eggs
- ¼ cup firmly packed brown sugar
- 2 tablespoons chopped green pepper, if desired
- 1 tablespoon chopped onion or 1 teaspoon instant minced onion
- 1 tablespoon prepared mustard
- ¼ cup milk or pineapple syrup

OVEN 350°   6 SERVINGS

In large mixing bowl, combine all ingredients; mix well. Press into 9x5-inch (2 qt.) loaf pan. Bake at 350° for 60 to 70 minutes. Let stand 5 minutes before removing from pan.

Tips: If desired, top unbaked ham loaf with ¾ cup (8½-oz. can) drained crushed pineapple mixed with 2 tablespoons brown sugar. Bake as directed.

For a Honey Glaze, mix 2 tablespoons honey with 2 tablespoons brown sugar; spoon over unbaked ham loaf.

Ham loaf is also good with 3 to 4 tablespoons orange marmalade or dark corn syrup spooned over before baking.

For miniature loaves, divide into 3 miniature pans or about eight 5-oz. custard cups; bake in miniature pans for 35 to 40 minutes; in custard cups for 25 to 30 minutes.

To make ahead, prepare and place in loaf pan; refrigerate or freeze. Allow to thaw and bake as directed.

TIMETABLE FOR ROASTING HAMS

Ham	Average Weight	Meat Thermometer Reading	Approx. Cooking Time per Lb.
(Cook before eating)			
Whole ham	10-14 lbs.	160°	18-20 min.
Half ham	5-7 lbs.	160°	22-25 min.
Shank or butt portion	3-4 lbs.	160°	35-40 min.
(Fully cooked or canned)			
Whole ham	10-14 lbs.	130°	10-15 min.
Half ham	5-7 lbs.	130°	18-24 min.
Shank or butt portion	3-4 lbs.	130°	18-24 min.
Picnic shoulder (Cook before eating)	5-8 lbs.	170°	35 min.
Picnic shoulder (Fully cooked)	5-8 lbs.	130°	25-30 min.

Casseroles bake to their best if they are centered in the middle of the oven.

Ham chunks glazed with spicy pie cherries, topped with parkerhouse biscuits make a great way to use leftover ham. A pretty Christmas supper, ready in about an hour and a quarter. Serve with a green vegetable and tossed salad.

SWEET CHERRY HAM BAKE

    4 cups cubed cooked ham
    1 cup (2 stalks) chopped
       celery
    ½ teaspoon dry mustard
    2 cups (1-lb. can) prepared
       cherry pie filling
    2 tablespoons brown sugar
    3 tablespoons lemon juice
    ⅛ teaspoon ground cloves

Parkerhouse Biscuits

    1½ cups Pillsbury All Purpose
       Flour*
    1 tablespoon sugar
    2 teaspoons baking powder
    ½ teaspoon salt
    ¼ cup shortening
    ⅓ cup milk
    1 egg
    1 to 2 tablespoons butter or
       margarine

OVEN 425°   6 SERVINGS

Combine ham, celery and dry mustard in 12x8-inch (2 qt.) baking dish. Combine cherry pie filling, brown sugar, lemon juice and cloves. Spoon over ham. Bake at 425° for 20 minutes. Place Parkerhouse Biscuits on hot mixture. Bake at 425° for 15 to 20 minutes until golden brown.

Parkerhouse Biscuits: Combine flour, sugar, baking powder and salt in mixing bowl. Cut in shortening. Combine milk and egg. Add to flour mixture; mix until dry particles are moistened. Knead on floured surface 12 strokes. Roll biscuits to ¼-inch thickness. Cut into rounds with floured 2½-inch cutter. Make a crease with dull edge of knife to one side of center. Place small pat of butter on larger portion. Fold small portion over butter; press to seal.

Tips: If desired, use 1 can (8 oz.) Pillsbury Refrigerated Quick Parkerhouse Dinner Rolls for Parkerhouse Biscuits. Bake at 400° for 15 to 20 minutes.

Or, omit Parkerhouse Biscuits and serve over rice.

*For use with Pillsbury Self-Rising Flour, omit baking powder and salt.

A delicious way to fix up ham. Serve with rice, broccoli and a tossed salad.

BAKED HAM SLICE IN ORANGE SAUCE

  1 smoked ham slice, cut
    1½-inches thick
10 to 12 whole cloves
  1 cup orange juice
  ½ cup firmly packed brown
    sugar
  1 tablespoon cornstarch
  ⅛ teaspoon ground ginger

OVEN 325°   4 TO 6 SERVINGS

Cut slashes in fat edge of ham slice. Insert cloves in fat. Place ham slice in baking dish or casserole. Combine remaining ingredients; pour over ham. Bake at 325° for 1½ to 2 hours, basting ham with sauce 4 or 5 times during baking. Cut into serving pieces.

Serve this oven-baked dish in 2 hours with baked potatoes and coleslaw.

BAKED HAM SLICE SPECIAL

  1 smoked ham slice, cut
    1½-inches thick
  ½ cup firmly packed brown
    sugar
  ½ cup dry bread crumbs
  2 teaspoons prepared
    mustard
  ¼ cup wine vinegar
1¼ cups apple cider or juice
    or other light fruit juice

OVEN 325°   4 TO 6 SERVINGS

Cut slashes in fat edge of ham slice. Place ham in baking dish. Combine brown sugar, bread crumbs, mustard, vinegar and ¼ cup of the apple juice. Spread mixture evenly over top of ham. Pour remaining 1 cup apple juice around ham Bake, uncovered, at 325° for 1½ to 2 hours until topping is crisp. Cut into serving pieces.

Center Cut Ham Slice: A slice cut crosswise through the center section of ham (unless cut from a boneless ham, it contains the round leg bone).

Bacon: Cut from the side of pork, cured and smoked. Available in slabs (unsliced) or already sliced, in varying thicknesses.

Canadian-Style Bacon: This cut is the boneless loin muscle (which would otherwise be a Loin Roast) that has been cured and smoked. It is available whole, cut into sections or sliced; it is also available "fully-cooked" or "cook-before-eating".

A delicious meat for brunch with eggs and rolls, or serve like you would ham for dinner.

GLAZED BAKED CANADIAN-STYLE BACON

1½ lbs. piece Canadian-style
    bacon
  ½ cup pickle relish, drained
  2 tablespoons honey
  ¼ teaspoon dry or prepared
    mustard

OVEN 325°   6 SERVINGS

Place meat in shallow baking pan. Cut meat, halfway through, into 6 slices. Combine pickle relish, honey and mustard; spoon between slices of meat. Bake at 325° for 1¼ hours until meat thermometer registers 160°, spooning juice over meat every 15 minutes during baking.

Tips: Canadian bacon is also good with any of the Ham Glazes, page 73; prepare half a recipe.

For other weights of Canadian bacon, allow to bake 35 to 40 minutes per lb. of meat.

For 2 to 3 servings, halve all ingredients. Prepare as directed.

PANFRIED CANADIAN-STYLE BACON:
Fry slices, ⅛ to ¼-inch thick, as directed for bacon. Allow 3 to 4 slices per serving.

BACON

PANFRIED BACON: Place bacon in large cold fry pan. Heat slowly, separating slices so that they lie flat in fry pan. Fry slowly 2 to 3 minutes. Turn slices and fry 2 to 3 minutes longer until bacon is crisp. Drain on paper towel.

OVEN COOKED BACON: Separate bacon slices and place on rack in shallow baking pan. Bake at 400° for 10 to 12 minutes until crisp.

BROILED BACON: Separate bacon slices and place on cold broiler rack. Broil 3 inches from heat for 3 to 4 minutes. Turn and broil 3 to 4 minutes longer until crisp, watching carefully.

Foods that can be made ahead and then warmed or reheated before serving offer a great convenience to busy, on-the-move cooks. Make it the night before; serve it hot at dinner-time. Or, make it early in the day; take it on a picnic.

Many of the details of meal preparation can be completed the night before or early that day. Molded gelatin salads or marinated salads can be prepared ahead of time and stored in the refrigerator until serving time. Frozen salads, too, help leave your last few minutes before meal time free from a frantic rush.

Vegetables can also be prepared — or at least organized ahead. Dishes that bake can occasionally be assembled, refrigerated and then baked just before dinner. Some vegetables can even be prepared entirely in advance and reheated later. For vegetables that need only a short cooking period, cleaning and trimming ahead of time can still cut down on your actual time in the kitchen.

Desserts lend themselves very well to make-ahead preparation. Cakes are naturals for this and so are pies. Gelatin desserts, pudding-type desserts, and any others that are frozen or chilled help to let you spend your time in the kitchen when you have it to spend — and let you enjoy your family or guests later.

The main dish usually forms the basis of the meal and frequently is the most time-consuming part of meal preparation. Some of your time before dinner can be free if the dish is one that bakes for a length of time (Roasts, Pot-Roasts, oven-prepared recipes) or if it is one that simmers unattended for a while.

If there's a premium on your time before dinner, recipes that can be partially made or assembled ahead and then completed right before dinner can make minutes work for you. Other dishes can be completely cooked in advance and refrigerated or frozen until you're ready to reheat them.

These types of recipes also add great convenience to take-along meals — whether the occasion is a pot-luck supper, a dish taken to a friend or the main feature of a picnic. Choose the container that you will take with its use in mind. If the dish is to be taken hot and served warm, a heavy container that will hold the heat well will give you the best results. If you plan to reheat the dish before serving (as we have done with this Hearty Ham 'N Bean Soup), a heat-proof container with a tight-fitting lid is great for transporting. Heat and serve from the very same container!

For our picnic in the woods, we've taken along a large container of Hearty Ham 'N Bean Soup that was prepared the day before.

A man-sized salami sandwich, dill pickle, and fruit complete our menu. Your take-along meals can include your own family's favorites.

The make-ahead Tips with the recipes in this book can give you additional latitude in your creativity and can help you get the details of a meal under control so that you can relax and enjoy the occasion, too.

A favorite for that chilly day! Serve it hot as a main dish with a salad and hot rolls for supper or serve it rewarmed as a snack.

HEARTY HAM 'N BEAN SOUP

2 cups (16-oz. pkg.) dry navy beans
6 cups water
2 lbs. ham shank
½ cup (1 small) chopped onion or 2 tablespoons instant minced onion
1 teaspoon salt
¼ teaspoon dry mustard
1 clove garlic, minced
6 peppercorns

6 TO 8 SERVINGS

Soak beans overnight in water. In large saucepan (5 qt.), combine beans in water with remaining ingredients. Simmer, covered, for 3 to 3½ hours until beans are tender. Remove peppercorns and ham bone; cut ham from bone into chunks and return to soup. If a smoother soup is desired, beans can be mashed or soup can be processed at medium speed in a blender.

Tips: If using a pressure cooker, beans do not need to be soaked overnight. Combine all ingredients and cook an extra 15 minutes at 15 pounds of pressure.

Soup can be made ahead and frozen up to 3 weeks or refrigerated for about a week.

Hearty Ham 'n Bean Soup, opposite page

Baked Ham Buffet

For holidays, special occasions, and any time the group is large, serve the meal buffet-style. Buffet service is well suited to large groups because seating can be extended beyond the table, and large serving dishes don't clutter the eating area. Since the guests serve themselves, the hostess is free to enjoy herself, too.

Lap trays and TV trays are a great convenience if the group is too large for the table. If there are enough TV trays for each person, they can even be set with napkins and silverware. Card tables are another answer to the seating question and can be decorated in conjunction with whatever theme you have chosen.

Arrange the buffet so that guests pick up their plates at the beginning of the buffet. The delicious dinner you've prepared comes next. Then other things, such as silverware and napkins, can be placed at the end of the line — guests won't have to juggle them while they're serving food for themselves. Beverages can be served individually once everyone has been served and is seated.

Ham fills the bill for a main dish that's popular and serves a lot of people. We've gone traditional in our menu and have served Candied Sweet Potatoes, Peas with Mushrooms and Onion, Molded Gelatin Salad with Grapefruit and Pears, and Hot Butterflake Rolls. The variety of accompanying dishes which could be served in this menu is endless. Foods served for a buffet should be easy to serve and easy to handle during eating. Keep in mind flavor and texture variety in selecting side dishes, and be conscious of colors and shapes that you're combining.

Dishes can be cleared from trays or card tables just as you would do for a seated dinner. Serve dessert to each guest individually or buffet style — whichever you choose. A warm pie topped with sweetened whipped cream or ice cream might complete this menu traditionally. You can choose the one that best complements the menu you've chosen.

Veal

Once available primarily in the spring, veal is now available in many markets on a year round basis. Veal is young beef, and because it is from young animals, it has a very mild flavor. Recipes which include a sauce, a stuffing or a coating help retain the natural juices and enhance the flavor. The mild flavor of veal opens many avenues of accompanying side-dishes for your meal planning. Strong and subtle flavors are equally at home. To compliment its tender texture, serve veal well-done.

When purchasing veal, look for light grayish-pink lean tissue that has a very fine grain, and is fairly firm and velvety in texture. It should have very little fat, and the bones should be red and porous. Veal is usually most plentiful in late winter to spring.

Veal Scallopini, page 85, and Buttered Noodles

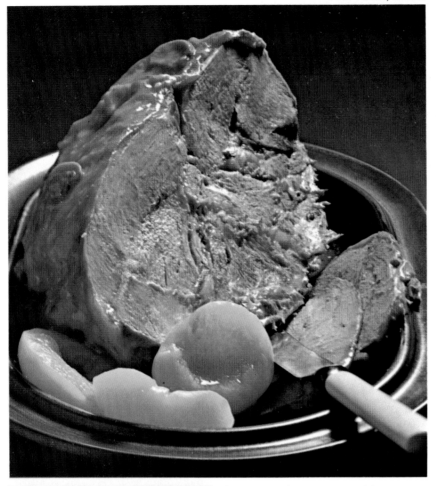

This apricot sauce adds a pretty, flavorful accent to veal roast. Allow about 2½ hours for roasting.

GLAZED VEAL ROLL

  3 lbs. boneless rolled veal
     shoulder or rump roast
 Salt
 Pepper
 1½ cups (12-oz. can) apricot
     nectar
  ½ cup firmly packed brown
     sugar
  1 tablespoon grated lemon
     peel
  1 tablespoon lemon juice
  ⅛ teaspoon ground cloves

OVEN 325°   6 TO 8 SERVINGS

Season meat with salt and pepper. Place on rack in open shallow roasting pan. Insert meat thermometer so the bulb reaches the center of the thickest part. (Do not add water; do not cover.) Roast at 325° for 1½ hours. Meanwhile, combine remaining ingredients in saucepan; simmer 10 minutes. Cool. After meat has roasted 1½ hours, spoon one-third of apricot glaze over meat every 20 minutes. Roast until well done, about 2½ hours total roasting time until meat thermometer registers 170°. If desired, serve drippings as sauce with meat.

VEAL ROASTS

Shoulder Roast: Includes several muscles and occasionally contains some rib bones on the underneath side. This cut is from the arm area and contains the round arm bone. It can be roasted or cooked with liquid.

Golden mushroom soup adds an easy sauce and flavor to a veal roast. Start cooking about 2½ hours ahead. Serve with warm rolls, green beans and an apple salad.

VEAL ROAST

  2½ to 3 lbs. veal shoulder,
     blade or rump roast
  1¼ cups (10½-oz. can) con-
     densed golden mushroom
     soup

OVEN 325°   4 TO 6 SERVINGS

Place roast, fat-side up, in a 2½ to 3-quart covered casserole. Pour soup over roast. Cover; bake at 325° for 2 to 2½ hours until tender. Serve sauce over roast. If desired, garnish with peach slices.

Tips: To cook on top of range, place in Dutch oven and simmer, covered, for 2 to 2½ hours until tender.

For added seasoning, add ½ teaspoon crushed leaf thyme, marjoram or ¼ teaspoon garlic powder or instant minced garlic.

Standing Rump Roast: A triangular-shaped roast that contains the rump bone, the tail bone and usually part of the round leg bone. It is from the rump area and may be boned, rolled, tied and called Rolled Rump Roast. It can be roasted or cooked with liquid.

A quick way to dress up leftover veal — add to a pineapple and almond sauce. Ready to serve in about 20 minutes.

VEAL ALMOND

2 tablespoons butter or margarine
2 chicken bouillon cubes or 2 teaspoons instant bouillon
2 cups water
2 tablespoons cornstarch
1 cup (8¼-oz. can) undrained crushed pineapple
2 to 3 cups cubed cooked veal
½ cup toasted slivered almonds
½ cup (1 stalk) sliced celery
1 teaspoon salt

6 SERVINGS

Melt butter in fry pan. Add bouillon and water; bring to a boil and reduce heat. Blend cornstarch and pineapple; add gradually to liquid, stirring constantly until mixture boils and thickens. Add veal, almonds, celery and salt. Bring to boil and simmer 5 to 10 minutes. Serve over chow mein noodles or rice.

Breast of Veal: Cut from the breast area and includes the rib bones. The bones are usually removed by the meat retailer if the breast is to be stuffed for roasting.

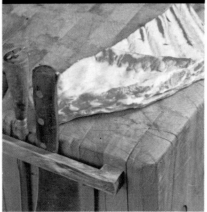

Dress up this economical cut of veal with a moist apple and sausage stuffing. Serve with baked potatoes, broiled tomatoes and coleslaw in 2½ hours.

SAUSAGE STUFFED BREAST OF VEAL

½ lb. pork sausage
¼ cup chopped onion or 1 tablespoon instant minced onion
1 cup soft bread cubes
1 small apple, peeled and chopped
1 tablespoon parsley flakes
½ teaspoon salt
½ teaspoon powdered sage or poultry seasoning
⅛ teaspoon pepper
2 tablespoons sherry or water
1 breast of veal (about 2½ lbs.)*

OVEN 325°   6 TO 8 SERVINGS

In fry pan, brown sausage and onion; drain off fat. Mix in remaining ingredients except veal. Place stuffing down center of veal. Roll up veal with stuffing inside; fasten with skewers or tie with string. Place in covered baking dish; brush with sausage drippings or butter. Cover; bake at 325° for 2 to 2½ hours until tender. Serve with pan juices.

Tip: *For ease in cutting and serving, have meat man remove bones.

CHOPS:

Loin Chops: Contains a T-shaped bone, portions of the loin muscle and the tenderloin muscle, and are covered by a thin layer of fat. They are from the loin area.

A flavorful dish that's quite low in calories. Serve this with rice, broccoli and a fruit salad. Takes about 1½ hours to prepare.

VEAL CHOPS IN WINE

2 tablespoons flour
½ teaspoon salt
¼ teaspoon garlic salt
¼ teaspoon pepper
4 veal rib or loin chops, cut ½-inch thick or 1 lb. veal round steak, cut into 4 pieces
1 tablespoon oil or shortening
1 small onion, sliced
½ cup sliced canned or fresh mushrooms
¼ cup chopped green pepper, if desired
1 cup (8-oz. can) drained tomatoes
½ cup white or red wine

4 SERVINGS

Combine flour, salt, garlic salt and pepper. Coat chops with flour mixture. In fry pan, brown meat on both sides in hot oil. Add onion, mushrooms, green pepper, tomatoes and wine. Cover; simmer 1 to 1¼ hours until meat is tender.

Tip: For 8 servings, double all ingredients.

Rib Chops: These cuts contain the rib bone and have only 1 muscle; they come from the rib area.

Apricot and orange add a tangy flavor to these veal chops. Start 1¾ hours ahead.

FRUITED VEAL CHOPS

  2 tablespoons flour
  1 teaspoon salt
  ⅛ teaspoon pepper
  6 rib or loin veal chops, cut ¾ to 1-inch thick
  2 tablespoons oil or shortening
  ¼ cup water
  1½ cups (1-lb. can) drained apricot halves
  4 to 6 tablespoons orange marmalade

6 SERVINGS

Combine flour, salt and pepper. Coat meat with seasoned flour. Brown on both sides in hot oil in large fry pan. Add water; cover and simmer 1 hour. Turn meat and place apricot halves on top. Spoon marmalade over all. Cover; simmer 30 minutes longer, removing cover during last 15 minutes.

Tips: To make ahead, place chops in shallow baking dish before topping with apricots and marmalade. Cool and refrigerate. Bake, covered, 30 minutes; uncover and bake 15 more minutes.
For 3 servings, halve all ingredients. Prepare as directed.

Arm Steaks: These can be identified by the round bone and the small amount of fat within the muscles. They are from the shoulder area, and are sometimes called Arm Chops.

Blade Steaks: These cuts contain the blade bone and are cut from the shoulder area. They are sometimes called Blade Chops.

Round Steaks: The round leg bone identifies these cuts. They are cut from the rump area and are usually cooked with liquid.

Moist apple stuffing is rolled inside pieces of veal to make flavorful individual servings for guests or family. Serve with broccoli and a fruit salad.

APPLE STUFFED VEAL BIRDS

  1 to 1½ lbs. veal round steak
  ⅓ cup flour
  1 teaspoon salt
  ¼ teaspoon pepper
  ½ cup soft bread cubes
  ¼ cup (½ stalk) chopped celery
  1 small apple, chopped
  2 tablespoons chopped pecans or walnuts, if desired
  ¼ teaspoon prepared mustard
  1 tablespoon dry sherry or water
  2 tablespoons oil or shortening
  1 chicken bouillon cube or 1 teaspoon instant bouillon
  1 cup water

4 SERVINGS

Remove bone and cut veal into 4 pieces. Combine flour, salt and pepper. Pound flour into veal with meat hammer or edge of a heavy saucer until all the flour mixture is used. In mixing bowl, combine bread cubes, celery, apple, pecans, mustard and sherry; mix well. Place ¼ of stuffing on each piece of veal and roll up with filling inside. Fasten with toothpicks. In fry pan, heat oil; brown meat on all sides. Add bouillon and water; cover and simmer for 1¼ to 1½ hours until meat is tender, adding additional water if necessary. Serve meat juices over meat.

Tips: If desired, use ¼ to ½ cup sherry for part of water.

To make ahead, prepare and simmer 30 minutes. Place in baking dish; cool and refrigerate. To serve, bake, covered, at 350° for 1 hour.

A quick recipe for veal with a wine and herb flavor that's ready in 20 minutes. Serve with a noodle casserole, broccoli and a fruit salad. Pictured on page 80

VEAL SCALLOPINI

1½ lbs. veal round steak, cut
  ¼-inch thick
¼ cup flour
1 teaspoon salt
⅛ teaspoon pepper
2 tablespoons butter or
  margarine
1 cup (8 oz. or ½ pt.) sliced
  canned or fresh mushrooms
¼ cup dry sherry
¼ cup water
1 to 2 tablespoons chopped
  chives
1 tablespoon lemon juice
¼ teaspoon leaf rosemary,
  tarragon or marjoram

4 TO 6 SERVINGS

Cut steak into 4 to 6 serving pieces. Combine flour, salt and pepper; coat meat with seasoned flour. Pound meat with meat hammer or the edge of heavy saucer until ¼-inch thick, sprinkling with flour mixture as needed. In a large fry pan, brown both sides of veal in hot butter until golden brown. Add mushrooms, sherry, water, chives, lemon juice and rosemary. Simmer, covered, for 10 minutes. Remove meat to platter and spoon sauce over meat.

Tips: If desired, omit sherry and increase water to ½ cup.
For 2 servings, halve all ingredients. Prepare as directed.

The star of this paprika veal stew is the Butter Crumb Dumplings, like floating puffs of dressing. An hour and a quarter dish. Serve with a crisp salad.

CALIFORNIA CASSEROLE

2 lbs. veal round steak, cut
  into 1-inch pieces
⅓ cup flour
1 teaspoon paprika
¼ cup cooking oil
½ teaspoon salt
⅛ teaspoon pepper
2¼ cups water
1⅓ cups (10½-oz. can)
  condensed cream of
  chicken soup
2 cups (1-lb. can) drained
  small whole onions

Butter Crumb Dumplings

2 cups Pillsbury All Purpose
  Flour*
1 tablespoon poppy seeds, if
  desired
4 teaspoons baking powder
1 teaspoon poultry
  seasoning
1 tablespoon celery seeds
1 teaspoon instant minced
  onion
½ teaspoon salt
¼ cup cooking oil
1 cup milk
¼ cup butter or margarine,
  melted
1 cup dry bread crumbs

OVEN 425°   6 TO 8 SERVINGS

Coat veal with mixture of flour and paprika; brown in oil in large fry pan. Add salt, pepper and 1 cup of the water (part onion liquid can be used). Simmer, covered, for 30 minutes until tender. Transfer to a 3-qt. casserole. Heat soup in fry pan used for browning meat. Gradually blend in remaining 1¼ cups water. Bring to a boil, stirring constantly. Add gravy to meat; top with onions. Top with Butter Crumb Dumplings. Bake uncovered at 425° for 20 to 25 minutes until golden brown.

Butter Crumb Dumplings:
Combine flour, poppy seeds, baking powder, poultry seasoning, celery seeds, onion and salt in large mixing bowl. Add oil and milk. Stir just until moistened. Drop rounded tablespoonfuls of dough into mixture of butter and bread crumbs; roll to coat well with crumbs.

*For use with Pillsbury Self-Rising Flour, omit baking powder and salt.

A long-standing favorite that has been short-cutted by using a convenience mix. Add a green vegetable and a crisp salad for a satisfying meal.

EASY VEAL PAPRIKA

1 lb. veal round steak, cut
  into 1-inch cubes
2 tablespoons flour
½ teaspoon salt
Dash pepper
2 tablespoons cooking oil
1¼ cups water
½ to 1 tablespoon paprika
1 package (6¼ oz.) noodles
  with sour cream and
  cheese sauce mix
⅓ cup water
½ cup milk
1 tablespoon butter or
  margarine

4 TO 6 SERVINGS

Combine flour, salt and pepper. Coat meal with flour mixture. Brown meat in oil in large fry pan. Reduce heat. Add 1¼ cups water and paprika. Simmer, covered, for 45 minutes until meat is tender. Add package of noodles and ⅓ cup water. Continue simmering, covered, stirring occasionally, 10 minutes until noodles are cooked. Combine milk, butter and package of sauce mix; stir to mix well. Pour over veal and noodle mixture. Simmer, stirring gently, until sauce thickens and mixture is bubbly. If desired, garnish with parsley sprigs.

Pre-breaded Patties: Several cuts of meat are available already coated with a crumb mixture, in ready-to-serve pieces. These cuts can be used in recipes in which the meat is breaded before cooking. Omit the ingredients used in breading and continue as directed.

Swiss cheese and ham hidden between thin slices of veal. Serve with a creamy vegetable and a green crisp salad.

VEAL CUTLETS CORDON BLEU

    12 veal cutlets, cut ¼-inch
       thick
       Salt
       Pepper
     6 slices Swiss cheese
     6 thin slices boiled ham
    ½ cup Pillsbury All Purpose
       Flour
    ¼ teaspoon ground nutmeg
    ¼ teaspoon ground cloves
     3 eggs, slightly beaten
     1 cup dry bread crumbs
    ¾ cup butter or margarine

                    6 SERVINGS

Pound veal with flat side of meat hammer or rolling pin until very thin. Sprinkle with salt and pepper. Place 1 slice cheese and 1 slice ham on each of 6 veal slices. Top with remaining veal. Pound edges together. Combine flour, nutmeg and cloves; dip both sides of cutlets into mixture and then into egg, and then crumbs. Brown 5 to 6 minutes on each side in hot butter in large fry pan until done.

Tip: If desired, prepare cutlets ahead and refrigerate until ready to fry.

Cutlets: These are thin, individual boneless pieces of veal that are usually cut from the round steak area but may also be cut from the shoulder area. See tips for making cutlets from round steak.

Veal and ham combine a mild and a strong-flavored meat. Seasonings and wine give it an elegant flavor. Try serving with baked potatoes, squash and a fruity salad.

VEAL AND HAM DUO

     1 lb. thinly cut veal steaks or
       cutlets*
    ½ to 1 lb. (8 to 16 oz.) thinly
       sliced boiled ham
    ½ teaspoon salt
    ¼ teaspoon pepper
    ¼ teaspoon leaf rosemary, if
       desired
    ½ cup white wine, sherry or
       water

OVEN 325°   4 TO 6 SERVINGS

In ungreased shallow casserole (about 2 qt.), alternate layers of ham and veal. Sprinkle with salt, pepper and rosemary. Pour wine over meat. Bake, covered, at 325° for 1 hour until veal is tender. Garnish with parsley. Serve.

Tips: *Veal cutlets can be made from veal round steak. Cut steak into 4 pieces. Flatten to ¼-inch thickness by placing between sheets of plastic wrap and pounding with flat side of meat hammer or rolling pin.

Leftover ham can be conveniently used in this recipe for the boiled ham.

Cubes of veal cooked in a savory sauce and served over noodles. Serve with peas and a colorful fruit salad in 1½ hours.

VEAL GOULASH

     3 tablespoons flour
    1½ teaspoons salt
    ⅛ teaspoon pepper
    1½ lbs. boneless veal, cut into
       1-inch cubes
     2 tablespoons oil or
       shortening
     2 cups water
     1 clove garlic
     1 teaspoon paprika
     1 teaspoon Worcestershire
       sauce
    ½ teaspoon celery seed, if
       desired
     2 tablespoons flour
    ¼ cup water

                    4 SERVINGS

Combine 3 tablespoons flour, salt and pepper. Coat meat with mixture. Brown on all sides in hot oil in large fry pan or Dutch oven. Add 2 cups water, garlic, paprika, Worcestershire sauce and celery seed. Cover. Simmer 1 hour until tender. Remove garlic. Blend 2 tablespoons flour and ¼ cup water until smooth. Stir into hot liquid. Cook, stirring constantly, until mixture boils and thickens. Serve over noodles.

Tips: To make ahead, prepare except for thickening with flour. Cool and refrigerate or freeze. To serve, reheat and thicken.

If desired, add 1 cup (8 oz. or ½ pt.) sliced fresh mushrooms after meat has browned; add ¼ cup white wine for part of water.

For 2 servings, halve all ingredients. Prepare as directed.

VEAL PARMESAN

½ cup grated Parmesan cheese
¼ cup dry bread or cracker crumbs
½ teaspoon paprika
¼ teaspoon salt
⅛ teaspoon pepper
4 veal cutlets*
1 egg, slightly beaten
2 to 3 tablespoons oil or shortening
4 slices or 1 cup shredded Mozzarella cheese, if desired
½ cup canned or 4 slices fresh tomato, if desired

4 SERVINGS

Combine Parmesan cheese, bread crumbs, paprika, salt and pepper. Dip veal into egg then into crumb mixture. In fry pan, heat oil; fry cutlets until golden brown on one side; turn. If desired, top browned side with Mozzarella cheese and tomato section. Reduce heat and continue cooking until veal is done and cheese has melted, about 10 minutes.

Tips: *If desired, buy 1 to 1½ lbs. veal round steak. Cut into serving pieces and flatten to ¼-inch thickness, placing between sheets of plastic wrap and pounding with flat side of meat hammer or rolling pin.

To make ahead, dip veal in egg and crumbs; refrigerate up to 3 hours, then start cooking 20 minutes before serving.

Ground Veal: Made by grinding meat and trimmings.

Under the golden soufflé is a savory mixture of veal and herbs. Serve hot from the oven in an hour and a half with a green vegetable and a fruit salad.

TOP HAT VEAL PIE

9-inch Unbaked Pastry Shell
1 lb. ground veal
2 tablespoons oil or shortening
1 tablespoon instant minced onion or ¼ cup chopped onion
1 to 2 bay leaves
1 cup water
1 tablespoon flour
1 tablespoon parsley flakes
1 teaspoon salt
⅛ teaspoon pepper
Dash ground thyme
Dash ground ginger
1 egg, slightly beaten

Cheese Soufflé

2 tablespoons butter or margarine
2 tablespoons flour
½ cup milk
1 cup (4 oz.) shredded Cheddar cheese
2 eggs, separated

OVEN 425°   5 TO 6 SERVINGS

Brown ground veal in oil in large fry pan. Add onion, bay leaf and water. Simmer uncovered for 15 minutes, stirring occasionally. Stir in flour, parsley, salt, pepper, thyme, ginger and egg. Pour into Unbaked Pastry Shell. Bake at 425° for 15 minutes while preparing Cheese Soufflé. Reduce oven temperature to 375°. Pour Soufflé over partially baked pie, sealing to edge of crust. Bake at 375° for 20 to 25 minutes.

Cheese Soufflè: Melt butter in medium saucepan. Blend in flour. Gradually add milk. Cook over medium heat, stirring constantly, until thickened. Add cheese; stir until melted. Remove from heat. Add egg yolks. Blend in thoroughly. In separate bowl, beat egg whites until stiff, but not dry. Gently fold into cheese mixture.

BREADED VEAL CUTLETS

2 tablespoons flour
½ teaspoon salt
¼ teaspoon ground cloves
⅛ teaspoon pepper
1 egg, slightly beaten
1 to 2 teaspoons Worcestershire sauce
4 to 6 veal cutlets*
½ cup dry bread or cracker crumbs
2 to 3 tablespoons oil or shortening

4 SERVINGS

Combine flour, salt, cloves and pepper. Add Worcestershire sauce to egg. Coat cutlets with seasoned flour; then dip in egg and then bread crumbs. In large fry pan, heat oil; brown cutlets on both sides until golden brown. Continue cooking over low heat 5 to 7 minutes until veal is done.

Tips: *If desired, buy 1 to 1½ lbs. veal round steak. Cut into serving pieces and flatten to ¼-inch thickness by placing between sheets of plastic wrap and pounding with flat side of meat hammer or rolling pin.

To make ahead, dip veal in egg and crumbs. Refrigerate up to 3 hours; then, start frying 15 minutes before serving.

Veal takes on a cheesy Italian flavor in this dish that's great for making ahead. Serve with a green vegetable, crisp salad and crusty bread.

VEAL PARMIGIANA

- ⅓ cup grated Parmesan cheese
- 2 tablespoons cornflake crumbs or dry bread crumbs
- 1 egg, slightly beaten
- 1 to 1½ lbs. veal cutlets or veal round steak, cut into 4 serving pieces
- 2 tablespoons oil or shortening
- ½ cup (1 med.) chopped onion
- 1 cup (8-oz. can) tomato sauce
- ¾ teaspoon salt
- ⅛ teaspoon pepper
- ⅛ teaspoon leaf oregano or Italian seasoning
- 4 oz. sliced or 1 cup shredded Mozzarella cheese

OVEN 375° 4 SERVINGS

Combine Parmesan cheese and crumbs on waxed paper. Dip veal in egg, then coat with cheese and crumb mixture. Brown in hot oil in large fry pan. Place in shallow baking dish (8-inch square or round). Add onion to fry pan and sauté until golden. Stir in tomato sauce, salt, pepper and oregano. Top pieces of veal with cheese, then pour tomato mixture over cheese, spreading to cover. Sprinkle with additional Parmesan cheese. Bake at 375° for 30 minutes until bubbly.

Tips: To make ahead, assemble in baking dish, cool and refrigerate. To serve, bake 35 to 40 minutes until heated through.

For 2 servings, halve all ingredients, except egg. Prepare as directed.

Pre-breaded veal patties can be used for the veal cutlets. Omit Parmesan cheese, cornflake crumbs and egg. Prepare as directed.

Veal Parmigiana offers an excellent opportunity to use an Italian theme for side dishes and table settings. Checkered tablecloths, candles, roses, violin music, and wine are all part of the romantic image of Italy. Any or all of these can be incorporated into your table setting — a romantic dinner for two or a hearty meal for ten.

Begin dinner with a salad and bread course. Crisp greens form the basis to which you can add all sorts of creative ingredients. Toss in raw vegetables or chilled cooked ones (a clever way to use leftovers); top with plain or flavored croutons for a crunch and added flavor. For a tasty dressing, choose vinegar and oil, Italian, Caesar, garlic, or your own favorite. Italian or French bread — served hot or cold, already sliced or whole — goes nicely with the salad.

The main course features Veal Parmigiana. We think Buttered Zuchinni Squash would taste good with this dish; you may have a vegetable favorite that you'd rather serve. Many different vegetable flavors can go well with this type of dish and add color variety as well. Serve the main course with more bread and butter; and if you like wine with a meal such as this, rosé and red wines are especially suited to these flavors.

Dessert can be ice cream, fruit combinations, filled meringues, a pie or a torte — or any of your favorites. For a European idea, you might try serving crackers and cheese or cheese and fruit with a dessert wine or coffee.

Lamb

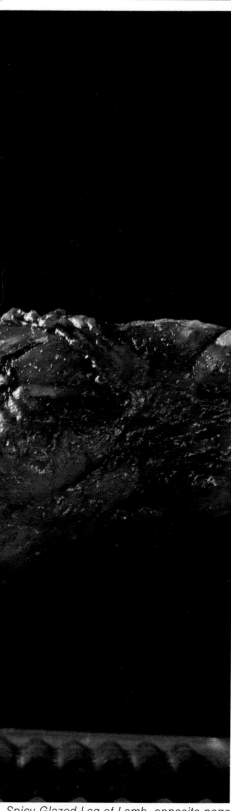

Lamb, also one of man's earliest animal foods, is frequently associated with religious traditions and holidays. For years it has been the chief meat in the Middle East, which accounts for the variety of lamb recipes which come from that region. It is also revered for its flavor in many other countries and holds note-worthy places in their cuisines. Lamb is frequently served with stuffings and sauces, of which mint is one of the most well known.

Lamb is a tender, flavorful meat that is best served very hot or chilled, rather than lukewarm. When broiling, roasting or grilling, it is usually cooked until medium to well done.

The color of lean lamb meat varies with the age of the animal, darker meat coming from the older animals and light pink meat coming from younger ones. The texture should be fine and velvety; fat should be smooth, firm and white. Lamb is most plentiful between January and March.

Leg of lamb is always popular. Add a special touch with one of the suggested glazes.

LEG OF LAMB

Place leg of lamb skin side down on rack in open shallow roasting pan. Season with salt and pepper. Insert meat thermometer so the bulb reaches the center of the thickest part of the leg, being sure the bulb does not rest in fat or on bone. (Do not add water; do not cover.) Roast at 325° to desired degree of doneness, adding one of the glazes during roasting, if desired.

TIMETABLE FOR ROASTING

Weight	Meat Thermometer Reading	Approx. Cooking Time per Lb.
5 - 8 lbs.	175-180°	30-35 min.
3 - 5 lbs.	175-180°	35-40 min.

Mint glazed leg of lamb: Melt mint jelly and spread over roast during last hour of cooking.

Garlic glazed leg of lamb: Combine ⅓ cup dry sherry, ⅓ cup water, 1 tablespoon paprika, ½ teaspoon leaf basil, 2 tablespoons soy sauce, 2 tablespoons cooking oil and 3 cloves garlic, minced; brush meat with glaze every 15 minutes during roasting.

Spicy glazed leg of lamb: Combine ¼ cup firmly packed brown sugar, 1 clove garlic, minced, 2 teaspoons salt, ½ teaspoon dry mustard, ½ teaspoon chili powder, ¼ teaspoon ground ginger, ¼ teaspoon ground cloves and 1 tablespoon lemon juice. Spread over meat during last 30 to 60 minutes of roasting.

Spicy Glazed Leg of Lamb, opposite page

LAMB

Leg of Lamb: The back leg section of the lamb. Available whole or cut into smaller sections; also available boned. Leg steaks are sometimes cut from the sirloin or center section.

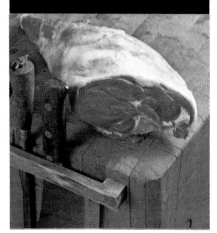

Next time try a boneless leg of lamb on the rotisserie. Time will vary from 3 to 5 hours depending on distance from coals and heat maintained during cooking.

Rib Roasts: Contain the rib bones and the back bones. These roasts are cut from the rib area, they are also called Lamb Rack.

Shoulder Roasts: These can be identified by their square shape; they contain the rib bones, blade bone, part of the arm bone and are covered with a layer of fat. They are sometimes boned and tied or rolled and sold as Rolled Shoulder Roasts.

BARBECUED LEG OF LAMB

3 to 4 lbs. boned leg of lamb
1 clove garlic, slivered
Salt
Pepper

6 TO 8 SERVINGS

Cut slits in leg of lamb, insert garlic slivers. Season with salt and pepper. Run spit through center of meat, making sure roast is evenly balanced. Insert thermometer at a slight angle so tip is in center of roast but not resting in fat or on rod. Roast until medium (175°) or well done (180°), brushing with melted mint jelly or prepared barbecue sauce during cooking.

How To Carve

Place the leg of lamb on the platter with the shank to the carver's right. Remove several slices from the thin side to form a solid base on which to set the roast.

TIMETABLE FOR ROASTING LAMB ROASTS
OVEN 325°

CUT	Weight	Meat Thermometer Reading	Approx. Cooking Time per Lb.
Boneless Leg	3-5 lbs.	175-180°	35-40 min.
Crown Roast	4-6 lbs.	175-180°	40-45 min.
Rib (Rack)	1½-2½ lbs.	175-180°	40-45 min.
Shoulder (bone in)	4-6 lbs.	175-180°	30-35 min.
Shoulder (cushion-style)	3-5 lbs.	175-180°	30-35 min.
Shoulder (rolled)	3-5 lbs.	175-180°	40-45 min.

Turn the roast on its base. Starting at the shank end, a small wedge cut is removed; then carve perpendicular to the leg bone as shown.

Release slices by cutting under them and along the leg bone, starting at the shank end. For additional servings, turn over to the original position and make slices to the bone, release and serve.

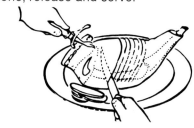

Cubes of lamb in a savory sour cream sauce. Serve over noodles in about 45 minutes.

Create a delightful new flavor experience with apples in a lamb curry. A two hour recipe. Note Tip for using leftover lamb.

A quick lamb curry made with soup. Serve in 45 minutes over rice along with favorite condiments and a refreshing fruit salad.

LAMB IN GOURMET SAUCE

2 lbs. lamb shoulder, cut into
  1-inch cubes
2 tablespoons oil or
  shortening
¼ cup chopped onion or
  1 tablespoon instant minced
  onion
¼ cup chopped green pepper
¼ cup flour
1 cup water
2 teaspoons salt
1 teaspoon crushed leaf
  tarragon
¼ teaspoon crushed leaf
  thyme
⅛ teaspoon pepper
½ to 1 cup dairy sour cream

6 SERVINGS

Brown meat on all sides in hot oil in large fry pan. Add onion and green pepper; brown 5 more minutes. Blend in flour. Add water, salt, tarragon, thyme and pepper. Cook, stirring constantly, until mixture thickens. Cover; simmer 30 minutes until tender. Reduce heat. Blend in sour cream. Heat, but do not boil. Serve over noodles.

Tips: To make ahead, prepare except for adding sour cream. Refrigerate or freeze. Reheat and stir in sour cream.

Use this idea for leftover lamb — do not brown the lamb; just add 2 to 3 cups cubed cooked lamb and 1 beef bouillon cube along with seasonings.

For 3 servings, halve all ingredients. Prepare as directed.

APPLE LAMB CASSEROLE

1 lb. lamb shoulder, cubed
⅓ cup Pillsbury All Purpose
  or Self-Rising Flour
2 tablespoons oil or
  shortening
2 cups water
1 large bay leaf
1 teaspoon salt
1 teaspoon parsley flakes
½ teaspoon ground thyme
¼ to ½ teaspoon ground
  curry powder
⅛ teaspoon pepper
1 small whole onion
2 cups (1-lb. 4-oz. can)
  sliced pie apples
2 tablespoons sugar
1 can (9.5 oz.) Pillsbury
  Refrigerated Hungry Jack
  Flaky or Flaky Buttermilk
  Biscuits

OVEN 425°   5 TO 6 SERVINGS

Coat lamb with flour. Brown in shortening in large fry pan. Stir in water, bay leaf, salt, parsley flakes, thyme, curry powder, pepper and onion. Cover and simmer 1 hour until meat is tender, stirring occasionally. Remove onion and bay leaf. Stir in apples and sugar. Bring to a boil. Transfer to 8 or 9-inch square (2 to 2½ qt.) baking dish.* Open can of biscuits; separate dough into 10 biscuits. Place around edge of baking dish. Continue baking at 425° for 15 to 18 minutes.

Tips: *If fry pan can be placed in oven, there's no need to transfer to baking dish.

If desired, 2 to 3 cups cooked cubed lamb can be used for the lamb shoulder. Omit browning.

If desired, use 3 cups chopped fresh peeled apples. Add to meat mixture last 20 minutes of simmering time.

If desired, omit biscuits. Continue simmering in fry pan for 15 minutes until apples are tender. Serve over rice.

QUICK LAMB CURRY

1½ lbs. boneless lamb shoulder,
  cut into 1-inch cubes
1 tablespoon oil or shortening
½ teaspoon salt
⅛ teaspoon pepper
1¼ cups (10½-oz. can) condensed cream of mushroom
  soup
1⅓ cups milk
2 teaspoons curry powder

6 SERVINGS

Brown meat slowly on all sides in oil in fry pan. Drain off fat. Sprinkle with salt and pepper. Combine soup, milk and curry powder. Stir into fry pan. Cover and simmer for 30 minutes until meat is tender. Serve over cooked rice.

Tip: Use this idea for leftover lamb — omit browning. Just add 2 to 3 cups cubed cooked lamb to soup mixture. Simmer 20 to 30 minutes.

CHOPS :

Loin Chops: The T-shaped bone in these chops divides the tenderloin and the rib muscle. They are cut from the loin area.

Rib Chops: These chops have only one muscle and usually contain one or two rib bones, depending on the thickness of the chops. They are from the rib area.

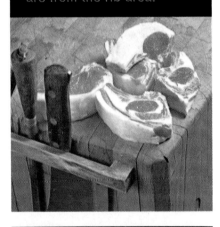

Shoulder Chops or Steaks: Tender chops containing several small muscles and the arm bone or blade bone.

Orange and soy sauce add a special flavor to these marinated lamb chops. Serve with rice and broccoli.

SOUTH SEAS LAMB CHOPS

 ½ cup cooking oil
 1 teaspoon salt
 2 tablespoons soy sauce
 2 tablespoons grated orange peel
 ⅓ cup orange juice
 6 shoulder lamb chops, cut 1-inch thick*

6 SERVINGS

Combine all ingredients except chops in shallow pan. Place chops in pan and marinate 2 hours, turning after 1 hour. Arrange chops on broiler rack. Place under broiler, 2 to 3 inches from heat. Broil 8 to 10 minutes until brown. Turn, brush with marinade and broil other side 6 to 8 minutes until brown.

Tips: *Try this marinade on other lamb chops — rib or loin chops, too. Allow extra time for broiling if they are thicker.

For 3 servings, halve all ingredients. Prepare as directed.

Try lamb shoulder chops braised in a savory mushroom sauce. Serve with minted peas and a fruit salad.

BRAISED LAMB CHOPS

 4 lamb shoulder chops*
 1 tablespoon oil or shortening
 ½ teaspoon salt
 ⅛ teaspoon pepper
 ⅛ teaspoon garlic powder or instant minced garlic
 ⅔ cup (4-oz. can) undrained mushroom stems and pieces
 2 tablespoons flour
 ½ cup water

ABOUT 4 SERVINGS

In large fry pan, brown chops in oil on both sides. Season with salt, pepper and garlic powder. Add mushrooms. Cover; simmer 45 to 60 minutes until tender. Remove chops to warm platter. Combine flour with water. Add to liquid in pan. Cook, stirring constantly, until mixture boils and thickens; serve over chops.

Tips: *Other chops (loin or rib) can be used for the shoulder chops.

If desired, 1¼ cups (10½-oz. can) condensed cream of mushroom soup can be added with mushroom stems and pieces. Continue as directed, omitting flour and water. Serve mushroom sauce over chops.

For 2 servings, halve all ingredients. Prepare as directed.

Broiled lamb chops are good anytime. Try plain or with one of the seasonings. We like the garlic marinade suggestion, too.

BROILED LAMB CHOPS

Set regulator to broil. Place lamb rib, loin or shoulder chops on broiler rack. Insert broiler pan and rack so the top of 1-inch chops is 2 inches from the heat and 2-inch chops is 3 inches from the heat. When one side is browned, season with salt and pepper, turn and finish cooking on the second side. (One-inch thick chops require 10 to 12 minutes, and 2-inch thick chops require 20 to 22 minutes total cooking time.) Season with salt and pepper.

Other seasonings for lamb chops: Add dash of garlic salt, paprika or curry powder when seasoning with salt and pepper.

Garlic marinated lamb chops: Combine ⅓ cup cooking oil, 1 teaspoon salt, 1 tablespoon vinegar, 2 cloves garlic, minced, and 1 bay leaf, crushed. Pour marinade over chops; marinate for 2 hours. Drain well and broil as directed.

For easy cleaning of broiler pans, the bottom and sides of the broiler pan can be lined with foil. For good broiling, the melted fats must be allowed to drain into the bottom of the pan. If foil is used to cover the rack, mold the foil to conform with the shape of the rack; make opening or slits in the foil to allow fats to drip off.

Broiled Lamb Chops, opposite page

Cubes of lamb and vegetables, alternated on skewers. Broil or barbecue and serve with rice or crusty rolls.

LAMB SHISH KABOBS

1½ cups (10-oz. pkg.) frozen Brussels sprouts
2 cups (8 oz. or 1 pt.) fresh mushrooms
3 firm tomatoes, cut into quarters
1 large cucumber
1½ lbs. boneless lamb shoulder, cut into 1½-inch cubes
½ lb. sliced bacon

Marinade

1 cup cooking oil
¼ cup lemon juice
2 cloves garlic, minced or ¼ teaspoon instant minced garlic
¼ teaspoon crushed leaf thyme

6 SERVINGS

Cook Brussels sprouts in boiling water in saucepan until almost tender; drain. Wash mushrooms, tomatoes and cucumber. Slice cucumber in half lengthwise, then cut into ½-inch pieces. Pour marinade over vegetables and meat in large bowl. Marinate for 1 hour.

Starting with bacon, thread meat and vegetables on skewers, interlacing bacon over and under pieces. Broil 5 inches from heat or grill over hot coals for 30 minutes, basting with marinade and turning occasionally until brown. Sprinkle with salt.

Marinade: Combine all ingredients; mix well.

Tips: For a quick marinade, use prepared Italian or French dressing.

For 2 to 3 servings, halve all ingredients. Prepare as directed.

Lamb curry makes an easy company dish. Serve with an assortment of condiments for spooning over the top. Add a refreshing fruit salad and relishes to complete your meal.

LAMB CURRY SUPREME

2 lbs. lamb shoulder, cut into 1-inch cubes
¼ cup butter or margarine
1 clove garlic, minced or ⅛ teaspoon instant minced garlic
½ cup (1 med.) chopped onion
¼ cup chopped celery
⅓ cup flour
2 teaspoons curry powder
1 teaspoon salt
3 cups chicken bouillon or 3 cups water and 3 chicken bouillon cubes
½ cup chutney, if desired
¼ cup chopped almonds, if desired
1 teaspoon prepared mustard
⅛ teaspoon pepper

6 SERVINGS

Brown meat on all sides in butter in large fry pan. Add garlic, onion and celery. Cook 5 minutes longer. Add flour, curry powder and salt. Mix well and cook 3 minutes. Add bouillon. Cook, stirring constantly, until mixture thickens. Add remaining ingredients. Cover. Simmer 45 minutes, stirring occasionally. Serve over rice with 3 of your favorite condiments: chutney, chopped nuts, shredded coconut, minced parsley, crumbled crisp bacon, thinly sliced green onions, sweet pickle relish, finely chopped hard-cooked egg, chopped preserved ginger, raisins or currants.

Tip: To make ahead, prepare and cook. Cool and refrigerate or freeze. Reheat to serve.

Tomato soup makes the easy sauce for these lamb rib pieces. Serve with rice or potatoes in about 2 hours.

LAMB RIBLETS IN TOMATO SAUCE

2½ lbs. lamb riblets
1 tablespoon oil or shortening
1 teaspoon salt
¼ teaspoon pepper
½ cup water
2 medium onions, sliced
½ cup (1 stalk) sliced celery
1 tablespoon brown sugar
1¼ cups (10¾-oz. can) condensed tomato soup
1 tablespoon flour
¼ cup water

6 SERVINGS

Brown meat on all sides in hot oil in large fry pan; drain off fat. Season with salt and pepper. Add ½ cup water, onions, celery, brown sugar and soup. Cover and simmer 1½ to 2 hours until tender. Remove to heated platter. Skim fat from drippings. Combine flour and ¼ cup water. Add to tomato sauce in fry pan; cook, stirring constantly, until mixture thickens. Serve over meat.

Tips: To make ahead, prepare and cook except for thickening with flour. Cool and refrigerate or freeze. To serve, reheat and thicken.

If lamb riblets are not available, use stew meat or lamb shoulder; cut into cubes.

For 3 servings, halve all ingredients. Prepare as directed.

Riblets: Riblets contain part of the rib bones and are cut from the breast section. The breast bone is removed and cuts are made between the ribs. They are sometimes sold as stew meat.

Lamb stew is always popular on a cool day. Ready in 1½ hours to serve with rolls and a crisp salad.

Make your own lamb patties or see the Tip for using the already prepared patties. Serve in 35 minutes with seasoned rice, buttered carrots and a crisp salad.

BEST-EVER LAMB STEW

    2 lbs. boneless lamb for stew, cut into 1-inch cubes
    ½ teaspoon sugar
    1 tablespoon oil or shortening
    2 teaspoons salt
    ¼ teaspoon pepper
    ¼ cup flour
    2 cups water
    ¾ cup dry red wine
    1 clove garlic, minced or ⅛ teaspoon instant minced garlic
    1 teaspoon Worcestershire sauce
    6 to 8 carrots, cut into pieces
    4 small whole onions, quartered
    4 celery stalks, cut into pieces
    2 to 3 potatoes, cut into pieces

6 SERVINGS

Sprinkle meat with sugar. Brown on all sides in oil in large fry pan or Dutch oven. Stir in salt, pepper and flour. Add water, wine, garlic and Worcestershire sauce. Cover; simmer 45 minutes until meat is tender, stirring occasionally. Add vegetables; cover and cook 30 to 45 minutes until vegetables are tender.

Tips: If desired, omit wine and use 2¾ cups water.

To make ahead, cook except for adding vegetables. Refrigerate or freeze. Reheat and add vegetables. Simmer 30 to 45 minutes until vegetables are tender.

For 3 servings, halve all ingredients. Prepare as directed.

GLAZED LAMB PATTIES

    1 lb. ground lamb
    2 tablespoons chopped onion or 2 teaspoons instant minced onion
    ½ teaspoon salt
    ¼ teaspoon paprika
    ⅛ teaspoon pepper
    1 tablespoon oil or shortening, if desired
    2 to 4 tablespoons mint jelly or prepared sweet and sour sauce
    1 tablespoon water

4 SERVINGS

Combine lamb, onion, salt, paprika and pepper; mix well. Shape into 4 patties. Brown on both sides in fry pan, using oil if desired; drain. Top patties with jelly; add water. Simmer, covered, 20 to 30 minutes turning occasionally to glaze patties.

Tips: Prepared lamb patties can be used. Brown on both sides, season with salt and pepper, top with jelly or sauce and add water; proceed as directed.

Patties can also be broiled or grilled; brush with melted jelly or sweet and sour sauce several times during broiling. (For 1-inch patties, broil 3 to 4 inches from heat for about 18 minutes totally. For thicker patties, broil 5 inches from heat for 22 total minutes.)

For 2 servings, halve all ingredients. Prepare as directed.

Stew Meat: Less tender sections of lamb cut into meaty pieces. They are made tender by simmering slowly in liquid.

Ground Lamb and Lamb Patties: Made by grinding lean meat and trimmings.

Lamb Shanks Dinner

Try this for your next company or special family dinner — hearty lamb shanks simmered in a flavorful wine sauce with colorful vegetables.

LAMB SHANKS WITH VEGETABLES

        4 lamb shanks
        1 tablespoon oil or shortening
     ½ cup (1 med.) chopped onion
    1½ teaspoons salt
     ½ teaspoon leaf tarragon or
          rosemary, if desired
        1 bay leaf
    1½ cups water
        1 cup red wine
        6 carrots, sliced
        2 cups (8 oz. or 1 pt.) whole
          fresh or canned mushrooms
    1½ cups (10-oz. pkg.) frozen
          peas
     ¼ cup flour
     ½ cup water

4 GENEROUS SERVINGS

In Dutch oven or large heavy saucepan, brown lamb shanks in oil. Add onion and brown slightly. Add salt, tarragon, bay leaf, 1½ cups water and wine. Cover and simmer 2 hours until tender. Add carrots and mushrooms; simmer 15 minutes. Add peas; cook 15 more minutes. Remove lamb shanks to heated platter; discard bay leaf. Combine flour and ½ cup water. Add to mixture in pan. Cook, stirring constantly, until mixture boils. Pour over lamb shanks; serve with noodles.

Lamb Shanks: These contain the leg bone and several muscles. They are usually cut from the front legs of lamb and require long simmering with liquid for tenderness.

Dinner for four — serve it at six o'clock, eight o'clock, ten o'clock or midnight. An intimate dinner with friends can be the beginning of a night on the town, a chance to spend the evening at home in the comfort of congenial conversation, or a relaxing way to end an elegant evening.

Lamb Shanks with Vegetables, served over noodles, is a full meal in itself. Complete the menu with a salad and some hearty rolls (purchase them already made or make them quickly with convenient mixes). To add crispness and flavor variety, we've served ours with an arrangement of cooked artichoke hearts and cooked egg slices on lettuce leaves. A salad like this can be arranged shortly ahead of time, covered and chilled in the refrigerator until serving time. Top it with dressing (we chose Italian) and a colorful garnish. For wine, the flavors in rosé and red wines offer the best choices.

After a hearty meal like this, serve a light dessert. Prepare a foreign coffee by topping strong coffee with a spoonful of sweetened whipped cream or whipped topping. Garnish with chocolate curls, a cinnamon stick, or ground cinnamon and nutmeg.

Good food is, of course, the basis for any meal; a friendly atmosphere contributes warmth and relaxation. Whether you enjoy entertaining on a casual or a more formal basis, having the details of the meal completed ahead of time allows you to relax and enjoy the meal, as well as your company.

Variety meats

Liver, Bacon and Onions, opposite page

Variety meats can open an interesting new area in main dishes. A variety of new food experiences awaits you in the many ways in which these meats can be prepared. Sauces and seasonings compliment their flavors and add an element of adventure to your meals.

Variety meats are usually good buys because they are excellent sources of many important nutrients and they are usually priced economically. Because no bone or fat is included in these meats, there is very little waste.

Available from beef, veal, pork and lamb, variety meats include heart, liver, kidneys, brain, tongue and sweetbreads. Each varies somewhat in flavor and tenderness; the price usually fluctuates with availability and demand.

A very easy, very thrifty dish. Use thick slices for broiling — you'll be surprised how tasty and tender these steaks will be!!

LIVER STEAKS

1 lb. liver, sliced ½ to 1-inch
   thick
¼ teaspoon salt
Dash pepper

4 SERVINGS

Place liver on broiler pan or cookie sheet. Broil 4 to 5 inches from heat for 3 minutes. Sprinkle with salt and pepper. Turn. Broil second side for 2 to 3 minutes until color just starts to turn. (Do not overcook; liver will toughen.) Cut into individual servings; serve immediately.

Tip: If desired, add one or several of the following to the second side before broiling:

1 tablespoon chopped bacon
   or bacon-flavored bits
2 teaspoons chopped onion
Dash curry powder
2 tablespoons tomato juice,
   white wine or sherry

Liver cooked in a sauce can be made quickly with a can of soup. Serve over rice or noodles along with cooked carrots and crisp wedge of lettuce.

SAUCY LIVER

1½ lbs. beef, veal, lamb or
   pork liver
¼ cup flour
1½ teaspoons salt
⅛ teaspoon pepper
¼ cup oil or shortening
1¼ cups (10½-oz. can)
   condensed cream of
   chicken, mushroom or
   celery soup
⅓ cup milk
¼ cup thinly sliced green
   onions or chopped onion

6 SERVINGS

Cut liver into serving pieces. Combine flour, salt and pepper. Coat meat with seasoned flour. Brown well on both sides in hot oil in fry pan. Blend soup with milk. Add soup mixture and onions to liver. Cover and simmer 15 minutes for veal, lamb or pork liver; 30 minutes for beef liver.

If your family likes liver, they'll love this served with mashed potatoes and a colorful salad or vegetables.

LIVER, BACON AND ONIONS

1½ lbs. beef, veal, lamb or
   pork liver
¼ cup flour
1 teaspoon salt
¼ teaspoon pepper
6 slices bacon
1½ cups (3 med.) sliced onions
½ cup water or red wine

6 SERVINGS

Cut liver into serving pieces. Combine flour, salt and pepper. Coat liver with seasoned flour. Fry bacon in fry pan until crisp; remove bacon and keep warm. Sauté onion and liver in bacon drippings. Add water; cover and simmer 15 minutes for veal, lamb and pork liver; 30 minutes for beef liver. Serve, topped with the crisp bacon.

Tip: For 3 servings, halve all ingredients. Prepare as directed.

A sparky tomato sauce lends a new flavor to liver. Spoon some of the extra sauce over mashed or boiled potatoes, and serve with a crisp salad and mild-flavored vegetable.

CREOLE LIVER

2 teaspoons butter or
   margarine
1½ lbs. calf or beef liver, cut
   into 1½-inch strips
½ cup (1 med.) chopped
   onion or 2 tablespoons
   instant minced onion
¼ cup chopped green pepper
½ teaspoon salt
⅛ teaspoon leaf marjoram or
   rosemary
⅛ teaspoon ground thyme or
   poultry seasoning
¾ cup (6-oz. can) tomato
   paste
½ cup condensed beef
   consommé*
¼ cup water

6 SERVINGS

In large fry pan, brown liver in butter on medium heat. Add remaining ingredients. Simmer, covered, 20 minutes for calf liver or 30 minutes for beef liver, adding small amounts of water if liquid becomes too thick. Serve hot.

Tip: *If desired, ½ cup water, 1 cube or 1 teaspoon beef bouillon and 1 teaspoon Worcestershire sauce can be used for the beef consommé.

Brains: Very tender and delicately flavored meat. They can be broiled, fried or cooked in liquid. Cook this cut immediately after purchase or precook until ready to use.

Sweetbreads: A tender and delicately flavored meat. They can be broiled, fried or cooked in liquid.

Sweetbreads are popular breaded and sautéed in butter. Serve with baked squash, spinach and a fruit salad.

PANBROILED SWEETBREADS

  2 quarts boiling water
  1 teaspoon salt
  2 tablespoons vinegar or
    lemon juice
1½ lbs. sweetbreads
  1 egg, slightly beaten
  ½ cup dry bread crumbs
  ¼ cup butter or margarine
  2 tablespoons minced
    parsley

6 SERVINGS

In saucepan, bring water, vinegar and salt to boil. Add sweetbreads. Reduce heat and simmer veal and lamb sweetbreads 25 minutes; beef sweetbreads 35 minutes. Drain; rinse in cold water until cool enough to handle. Slip thin membrane off with fingers. Remove any dark veins or thick tissue. Cut sweetbreads in half. Dry thoroughly. Dip in egg, then in crumbs. Brown on both sides in butter in large fry pan. Sprinkle with parsley.

Tip: To make ahead, simmer and coat with crumbs; cool and refrigerate or freeze. Fry just before serving.

Soup makes a quick and easy sauce for parboiled sweetbreads. Add color with a vegetable and crisp salad.

CREAMED SWEETBREADS

1½ lbs. sweetbreads
1¼ cups (10½-oz. can)
    condensed cream of
    mushroom soup
  ⅓ cup milk
  ¼ cup chopped chives or
    green onion
  Dash Tabasco sauce

4 SERVINGS

Follow directions for parboiling sweetbreads and cleaning Panbroiled Sweetbreads (below). Combine remaining ingredients in saucepan. Cut sweetbreads in thirds and add to sauce. Heat and serve over buttered toast.

Heart: A flavorful but less tender cut, so should be cooked in liquid.

Heart is good warm or cold, so cook enough for leftovers, too.

COOKED HEART

  1 beef or 2 veal, lamb or
    pork hearts
  2 tablespoons salt
  ¼ teaspoon powdered or
    1 teaspoon leaf thyme
  1 medium onion, sliced
  2 to 3 tablespoons vinegar,
    if desired

4 TO 6 SERVINGS

Remove white tubes from heart; wash. Place in large saucepan along with remaining ingredients; cover heart with water. Bring to boil; reduce heat and simmer until tender (beef 3 to 3½ hours; pork, veal and lamb, 2 to 2½ hours). Remove heart from broth and cut into slices to serve. Or, chill and cut into thin slices.

Dress up heart with a savory stuffing. Serve with creamed corn and a colorful salad.

STUFFED HEART

  1 beef heart or 2 veal hearts
  4 slices bacon

Stuffing

  2 cups dry bread cubes
1½ teaspoons instant minced
    onion
  1 teaspoon salt
  ½ teaspoon powdered sage
    or thyme
  Dash pepper
  3 tablespoons water
  2 tablespoons butter or
    margarine, melted

OVEN 325°   6 SERVINGS

Cook heart as directed for Cooked Heart (above). Meanwhile prepare Stuffing. Drain heart and stuff cavity with Stuffing; secure with string or skewers. Place in shallow baking dish; cover with slices of bacon. Bake, uncovered, at 325° for 40 to 45 minutes until bacon is crisp and heart is heated through. To serve, cut into slices.

Stuffing: Combine all ingredients; mix well.

Tips: If desired, use the seasoned bread cubes in the stuffing, omitting salt and sage.

To make ahead, simmer heart; cool and refrigerate. Stuff just before baking. Bake as directed for 45 to 50 minutes.

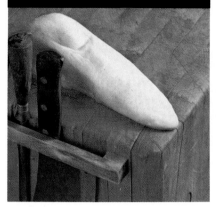

Tongue: A less tender meat that needs long, slow cooking in liquid. It is available fresh, pickled, corned, smoked or canned.

Serve cooked tongue hot today, then chill the leftovers for sandwiches or add to a hearty macaroni salad.

COOKED TONGUE

  1 fresh beef or 2 veal tongues
  6 to 8 peppercorns or ¼ teaspoon pepper
  1 small onion, sliced
  1 tablespoon (3 tsp.) salt
  1 bay leaf

6 TO 8 SERVINGS

In large saucepan, combine all ingredients; cover tongue with water. Bring to boil; reduce heat and simmer until tender (fresh beef tongue 3 to 4 hours; fresh veal tongue 2½ to 3½ hours). Remove tongue; cool slightly.

Cut off any bones or gristle. Slit skin on under side. Loosen with a paring knife and peel off skin from thick end to tip. To serve hot, slice ¼-inch thick. For cold tongue, chill thoroughly and cut into thin slices.

Tip: To cook smoked or cured tongue, omit salt and spices; cover with water and cook as directed.

Kidneys: Veal and lamb kidneys are sometimes attached to chops and sold as Veal Kidney Chops or Lamb English Chops. Veal, pork and lamb kidneys can be broiled or cooked in liquid. Beef kidneys are less tender, so should be cooked slowly in liquid.

A wine-flavored sauce gives a tremendous flavor to veal kidneys. A crisp salad and a mild flavored vegetable would be great partners for this dish.

KIDNEYS IN BURGUNDY SAUCE

  1 lb. veal kidneys
Hot water
  1 teaspoon salt
  2 tablespoons flour
  ¼ teaspoon salt
  2 tablespoons butter or margarine
  ½ cup water
  ½ cup Burgundy or red wine

4 TO 6 SERVINGS

Remove white membrane and hard parts from kidneys; cut into bite-sized pieces. Cover with hot water and 1 teaspoon salt. Let stand for 15 minutes; drain. Combine flour and ¼ teaspoon salt; coat kidney pieces with flour mixture. Brown in fry pan over medium heat. Add remaining flour, water and Burgundy, stirring until mixture thickens and comes to a boil. Reduce heat; simmer, covered, for 20 to 30 minutes until flavors have blended. Serve over noodles.

Tip: Other kidneys can be used for the veal kidneys. Simmer beef kidneys 45 minutes.

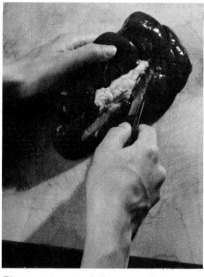

These are especially easy when part is prepared ahead. Serve with green beans, warm bread and sliced tomatoes.

BACON-WRAPPED BAKED KIDNEYS

  6 veal or lamb kidneys
  1 egg, slightly beaten
  ½ teaspoon salt
  ½ teaspoon garlic salt
  1 tablespoon Worcestershire sauce
  ½ cup dry bread crumbs
  6 bacon slices, cut in half crosswise

OVEN 400°   6 SERVINGS

Wash kidneys and cut in half. Remove outer membrane, white veins and fat. Place in saucepan. Cover with water and simmer for 35 minutes until tender; drain. Combine egg, salt, garlic salt and Worcestershire sauce in small bowl. Dip kidneys into egg mixture and then roll in bread crumbs. Wrap each kidney with bacon; fasten with toothpick. Place in shallow baking pan. Bake at 400° for 30 minutes until bacon is crisp and kidneys are brown.

Tips: To make ahead, coat kidneys with bread crumbs, wrap in bacon and place in baking pan. Cover and refrigerate. Bake just before serving.

Or, coat kidneys with crumbs and freeze. Thaw in refrigerator, wrap in bacon and bake as directed.

Sausages and luncheon meats

The process of sausage making was originally used as a means of preserving meats. Many combinations of ingredients were developed in various countries, and some of them have been named after the places of their origin (frankfurters — Frankfurt, Germany; bologna — Bologna, Italy; Vienna sausages — Vienna, Austria). They can be an interesting addition to your menus — for breakfast or dinner, as a snack or as a main dish.

Sausages and ready-to-serve meats are usually made of ground beef, pork, lamb, veal, or a combination of these. The meats used in making sausages are of the highest quality and are selected according to a ratio of lean to fat. After spices or condiments are added to the meat, it is placed in casings or pans for cooking, smoking and/or curing. All sausages and ready-to-serve meats can be left in their original wrappings or containers and should be stored in the refrigerator.

Fresh Sausage: These sausages are neither cooked nor cured and therefore must be cooked thoroughly before serving.

Fresh Pork Sausage: Made of selected fresh pork with spices added. It is available in links, patties, rolls and bulk.

Fresh Country-Style Sausage: Selected fresh pork with spices added. This is ground more coarsely than Fresh Pork Sausage. It is generally linked in casings but is sometimes sold in bulk.

Fresh Sausage Meat: Usually made of pork with spices added; however, it may — depending on quality — contain a percentage of beef and tripe also.

Bratwurst: A fresh sausage of coarsely ground beef and pork. It is flavored with spices and made into links. This sausage is a favorite for outdoor grillings.

Cooked sausage: (cooked and ready to serve)

Liver Sausage: A cooked mixture of finely ground pork and livers. It is mildly seasoned and may be smoked after cooking or may include smoked meat such as bacon.

Blutwurst or Blood Sausage: A cooked sausage made of diced, cooked pork fat, finely ground cooked meat and gelatin mixed with beef blood and spices. It is sold in rolls or links.

1 Bratwurst
2 Blutwurst
3 Liver Sausage
4 Fresh Pork Sausage
5 Fresh Country Style Sausage
6 Fresh Sausage Meat

HUNGRY JACK WIENEROLLAS

- 1 can (9.5 oz.) Pillsbury Refrigerated Hungry Jack Flaky or Buttermilk Flaky Biscuits
- ½ cup catsup
- 1 tablespoon chili seasoning mix
- 10 wieners (1¼ lb.)
- ¾ cup (3 oz.) shredded Monterey Jack, Mozzarella or Cheddar cheese
- ¾ cup finely chopped onion or 3 tablespoons instant minced onion
- 2 cups finely crushed barbecued potato chips

OVEN 400°   10 SANDWICHES

Separate dough into 10 biscuits. Roll or pat out each to a 7x3½-inch rectangle. Combine catsup with chili seasoning mix. Spread about 1½ teaspoons of mixture down center of each rectangle. Cut a lengthwise slit in each wiener; place cut-side up on dough. Fill slit with a tablespoon of cheese and a tablespoon of onion. Close wieners; wrap dough around each, pressing edges to seal. Brush lightly with water; roll in crushed chips. Place seam-side down on ungreased cookie sheet. Bake at 400° for 15 to 20 minutes until golden brown. Serve hot.

Tips: If desired, use ⅓ cup chili sauce for the catsup and chili seasoning mix.

Use your favorite kind of potato chips for the barbecued potato chips.

To make ahead, prepare, cover and refrigerate for 2 to 3 hours; bake as directed for 20 to 25 minutes.

CORNY WIENER CHOWDER

- 1 tablespoon butter or margarine
- 1 lb. wieners
- 1 cup (2 stalks) sliced celery
- 2 cups (1-lb. 1-oz. can) cream-style corn
- 1¼ cups (10½-oz. can) condensed cream of celery or potato soup
- 1 cup milk
- ½ tablespoon Worcestershire sauce
- ½ teaspoon salt

6 SERVINGS

In large saucepan, fry wieners and celery in butter until celery is tender. Add remaining ingredients. Simmer, covered, 15 to 20 minutes until heated through and flavors are well blended. If desired, garnish with paprika or pimiento.

Tip: If desired, 2 cups chopped cooked ham can be used for the wieners.

FRANKLY SAUERKRAUT

- 1 lb. (8) wieners (frankfurters)
- 2 cups (1-lb. can) drained sauerkraut
- ¼ cup chopped green pepper
- 1 tablespoon brown sugar
- 1 tablespoon chopped pimiento, if desired

OVEN 350°   8 SERVINGS

In ungreased 2 or 2½-quart casserole, combine all ingredients. Bake, covered, at 350° for 20 minutes until heated thoroughly.

Tip: Frankly Sauerkraut can be mixed ahead, covered and refrigerated. When ready to serve. heat as directed.

CHEESE 'N FRANK CRESCENTS

- 1 can (8 oz.) Pillsbury Refrigerated Quick Crescent Dinner Rolls
- 8 frankfurters or wieners
- 8 strips Cheddar or American cheese

OVEN 375°   8 CRESCENTS

Separate crescent roll dough into 8 triangles. Cut a narrow slit, lengthwise, in 8 frankfurters; insert strip of cheese in each. Place on wide end of crescent triangle; roll up. Place on ungreased cookie sheet, cheese side up. Bake at 375° for 10 to 15 minutes until golden brown.

Tips: Try spreading slit frankfurter with mustard before inserting cheese. If desired, brush rolls with barbecue sauce before baking.

QUICK MEXICAN WIENERS

- 4 wieners, sliced diagonally ¼-inch thick
- 2 cups (15-oz. can) chili with beans
- 1 teaspoon prepared mustard
- ¼ cup catsup or chili sauce
- 1 cup (4 oz.) shredded Cheddar cheese
- 2 cups corn chips

4 TO 5 SERVINGS

In medium saucepan, combine all ingredients except corn chips and ¼ cup of cheese. Simmer 10 minutes. Stir in corn chips; immediately pour into serving dish and sprinkle with remaining cheese. Serve immediately.

Tip: For 2 to 3 servings, halve all ingredients. Prepare as directed.

Shaped like a wagon-wheel in a pie pan and served in "spoked" wedges. Round-up time in one hour.

CHUCKWAGON ROUND-UP

- ¾ cup Pillsbury All Purpose Flour**
- 1½ teaspoons baking powder
- ½ teaspoon salt
- ¼ teaspoon chili powder
- ⅓ cup milk
- 2 tablespoons cooking oil
- 1 egg
- 1 lb. wieners*
- 2 cups (1-lb. can) undrained barbecue beans
- ½ cup (2 oz.) shredded Cheddar cheese
- 2 tablespoons dairy sour cream, if desired
- ½ teaspoon onion powder or 1 teaspoon instant minced onion
- ½ teaspoon leaf oregano, if desired

OVEN 375°   4 TO 6 SERVINGS

Grease 9-inch pie pan. Combine flour, baking powder, salt and chili powder in mixing bowl. Combine milk, oil and egg. Add to dry ingredients all at once, stirring until well mixed. Spread on bottom and sides of 9-inch pie pan. Reserve 2 wieners; cut remainder in ½-inch slices. Combine with beans, cheese, sour cream, onion powder and oregano. Spoon filling into center of dough in pie pan. Cut the two reserved wieners in half lengthwise and then crosswise. Place over filling, skin-side up, in spoke fashion. Bake at 375° for 30 to 35 minutes. Let stand 10 minutes before cutting into wedges and serving.

Tips: *If desired, fully cooked, smoked wieners or sausages can be used for the wieners.

**For use with Pillsbury Self-Rising Flour, omit baking powder and salt.

Wieners and other sausages are great for roasting over the fire. Winter or summer, hot, sizzling wieners are easy to take along and satisfy hungry outdoor appetites.

A quick lunch or supper idea for dressing up wieners with a barbecue sauce. Serve with Waldorf salad and lots of relishes in just 30 minutes.

BARBECUED WIENERS

- 1 lb. wieners
- 1 medium onion, sliced
- 1 tablespoon butter or margarine
- 1 package (⅝ oz.) Pillsbury Brown Gravy Mix
- 1 cup water
- 1 cup catsup
- 1 tablespoon prepared mustard
- ½ teaspoon Worcestershire sauce

4 TO 6 SERVINGS

Cut wieners diagonally into ½-inch slices. Lightly brown wieners and onion in butter in medium fry pan. Add gravy mix and water; stir until smooth. Mix in remaining ingredients. Cover and simmer 10 to 15 minutes. Serve over wiener or hamburger buns, or mashed potatoes.

Wieners in a spicy barbecue sauce. These will be a favorite treat for your children. Easy to make on a hurried evening.

SNAPPY WIENERS

- ¾ lb. (6) wieners
- 1½ tablespoons catsup
- 1 tablespoon cider vinegar
- 1 tablespoon instant minced onion or ¼ cup (½ med.) chopped onion
- 2 teaspoons Worcestershire sauce
- ¾ teaspoon horseradish, 1 tablespoon prepared mustard or 1 teaspoon dry mustard

OVEN 350°   6 SERVINGS

Score wieners diagonally. Place in ungreased 1½-quart baking dish. In small mixing bowl, combine remaining ingredients; mix well. Pour over wieners. Bake, covered, at 350° for 30 minutes. Serve hot.

Tip: To prepare in saucepan, heat over medium heat for 10 to 15 minutes until heated through.

HOT DOG S'MORES

2 cups Pillsbury Hungry Jack Mashed Potato Flakes
1 tablespoon butter or margarine, melted
1 lb. wieners
1 egg, slightly beaten
4 to 5 slices American or Cheddar cheese

OVEN 400°   6 SERVINGS

Combine ¼ cup of potato flakes with butter. Split wieners in half lengthwise. Place half of wieners on cookie sheet, cut side up, with sides touching. Prepare 4 servings mashed potatoes as directed on package, decreasing water to ¾ cup; stir in egg. Spread potatoes over wieners; top with 2 to 3 slices cheese. Cover with remaining wieners. Top with remaining cheese and sprinkle with buttered potato flakes. Secure with toothpicks. Bake at 400° for 15 to 20 minutes until golden brown.

Tip: These can be prepared ahead and refrigerated. Bake as directed for 20 minutes.

POLISH SAUSAGE AND SAUERKRAUT

4 cups (1-lb. 12-oz. can or 1 qt.) sauerkraut
1 medium apple, chopped
¼ cup firmly packed brown sugar
¼ cup water
½ teaspoon caraway seed, if desired
1 to 1½ lbs. Polish sausage or ring bologna

4 TO 6 SERVINGS

In saucepan, combine all ingredients except sausage; place sausage on top. Cover and simmer 30 minutes until heated through.

BOLOGNA AND CABBAGE SUPPER

½ to 1 medium head cabbage, shredded
¼ cup water
½ teaspoon salt
1 ring (about 12 oz.) bologna
1¼ cups (10¾-oz. can) condensed Cheddar cheese soup
2 tablespoons prepared mustard

5 TO 6 SERVINGS

In large saucepan, cook cabbage with water and salt, covered, over medium heat until tender, about 10 minutes. Drain; top with bologna. Combine soup and mustard; spoon over bologna. Cover and simmer 15 to 20 minutes until bologna is heated through.

Tip: This is also good with wieners in place of bologna.
For 2 to 3 servings, halve all ingredients. Prepare as directed.

ORANGE-GLAZED LUNCHEON LOAF

12-oz. can luncheon meat
4 thin orange slices, cut in half
8 whole cloves
¼ cup orange marmalade
1 teaspoon flour
⅛ teaspoon dry mustard or ¼ teaspoon prepared mustard

OVEN 350°   4 SERVINGS

Place luncheon meat in small shallow baking pan. Cut meat, halfway through, into 8 slices. Insert orange slices in slashes and 1 whole clove in each section of meat. Combine marmalade, flour and mustard. Spread glaze over loaf. Bake at 350° for 20 to 30 minutes until heated through and glazed.

Tip: Fix luncheon loaf early, then, bake just before serving.

EASY CORNED BEEF GAELIC

4 cups (½ med. head) shredded or chopped cabbage
3 cups cubed cooked corned beef*
1⅓ cups (10½-oz. can) condensed cream of celery or mushroom soup
½ cup milk
1 teaspoon salt
½ teaspoon caraway seeds
⅛ teaspoon pepper
1 can (8 oz.) Pillsbury Refrigerated Buttermilk Biscuits

OVEN 400°   6 SERVINGS

Combine cabbage, corned beef, soup, milk, salt, caraway seeds and pepper in 2-quart casserole. Cover. Bake at 400° for 30 minutes until hot and bubbly. Separate roll of biscuits into 10 biscuits. Cut each into quarters. Place cut pieces on top of casserole. Bake uncovered at 425° for 15 to 20 minutes until biscuits are golden brown. Garnish top with sprigs of parsley and pieces of pimiento.

Tip: *If desired, 2 cups (12-oz. can) luncheon meat, cubed, can be used for the corned beef. Decrease salt to ½ teaspoon.

PIE A LA ITALIANA

- 1 can (8 oz.) Pillsbury Refrigerated Quick Crescent Dinner Rolls
- 2 cups (8 oz.) Italian or Monterey Jack cheese, cut into ½-inch cubes
- 1 package (12 oz.) smoked sausages, cut into ¼-inch slices*
- ⅛ teaspoon salt
- ⅛ teaspoon pepper
- 1 tablespoon grated Parmesan cheese
- 2 eggs, slightly beaten

OVEN 325°   9-INCH PIE

Open can of rolls; unroll dough and separate into 8 triangles. Place 5 triangles in ungreased 9-inch pie pan pressing pieces together to form a crust. Reserve 3 triangles for top crust. Combine remaining ingredients in large mixing bowl. Pour into crust. Roll out each remaining triangle so longest side is 9 inches. Cut into ½-inch strips. Crisscross strips over filling to form a lattice top. Flute edge. Bake at 325° for 60 to 70 minutes until knife inserted 2 inches from edge comes out clean. Do not overbake. Cool 10 minutes before cutting into wedges.

Tip: *If desired, 2 cups (12-oz. can) luncheon meat, cut into ½-inch cubes, can be used for the smoked sausages.

REUBEN CASSEROLE

- 4 cups (1-lb. 11-oz. can) drained sauerkraut
- 2 medium tomatoes, sliced
- 2 tablespoons Thousand Island Dressing
- 3 cups thinly sliced cooked corned beef*
- 2 cups (8 oz.) shredded Swiss cheese
- 6 crisp rye crackers, crushed
- ¼ teaspoon caraway seeds, if desired
- 2 tablespoons butter or margarine, melted

OVEN 425°   6 TO 8 SERVINGS

Spread sauerkraut in bottom of 12x8-inch or 9-inch square (2 qt.) baking dish. Top with tomato slices; dot with dressing. Cover with corned beef; sprinkle with cheese. Combine crackers, caraway seeds and butter. Sprinkle mixture over casserole. Bake at 425° for 30 to 40 minutes until bubbly and cheese is melted. If desired, garnish with parsley.

Tip: *If desired, two 4-oz. pkgs. sliced corned beef can be used for the cooked corned beef. Or, 3 cups leftover cubed cooked corned beef can be used.

Pie A La Italiana, above

Cooked Smoked Sausage (ready to serve): These meats are both cooked and smoked. Even though they are ready to eat when purchased, the flavor of some is enhanced by heating before serving.

1 **Wieners:** Also called frankfurters, franks and Vienna-style sausage. Wieners are cured, spiced, packed in casings, smoked and cooked.

Several types of wieners are available: all beef, all meat (made with a combination of beef, pork, and/or veal), and wieners with cereal and/or nonfat dry milk added. Manufacturers are required by law to list the ingredients which are added, so the labels tell you exactly what you are buying.

2 **Bologna:** A cooked, smoked sausage made of beef and pork with mild seasonings similar to wieners. It is available in rings, rolls or slices.

3 **Lebonon Bologna:** A heavily smoked, semidry sausage of coarsely chopped beef.

4 **New England Style:** A cooked, smoked sausage of coarsely chopped, cured, lean pork with a ham flavor.

5 **Berliner:** Made primarily of coarsely ground cured pork and beef. They are seasoned with sugar and salt and is available in rolls or slices.

6 **Vienna Sausages:** Made with ingredients similar to wieners that are lightly seasoned, smoked and canned in about 2-inch lengths.

7 Knackwurst (Knoblauch): A cooked, smoked sausage of beef and pork, usually flavored with garlic. It is available in natural casings or skinless.

8 Smoked Links: Coarsely ground beef and pork that is seasoned with black pepper, fully cooked and heavily smoked. It is available in regular or cocktail sizes, and either in casings or skinless.

9 Braunschweiger: Liver Sausage which has been smoked.

Uncooked Smoked Sausage: Although these sausages have been smoked, they have not been cooked, and so must be cooked thoroughly before serving.

10 Smoked Country-Style Pork Sausage: Like fresh pork sausage, only mildly cured and smoked.

11 Mettwurst: Made of cured beef and cured pork. It is spiced, ground and packed into casings 1½ inches or more in diameter.

12 Polish Sausage or Kielbasa: Coarsely ground lean pork with beef added. It is cured, highly seasoned with garlic and smoked. It comes in links either 4 to 5-inches or 8 to 10-inches long and 1½-inches in diameter.

13 Smoked Country-Style Sausage: Coarsely ground pork and beef, mildly cured and smoked. It is usually sold in casings. Similar to Fresh Pork Sausage.

Sausages and luncheon meats are naturals for sandwiches — packed in lunchboxes or served buffet-style for luncheons. A selection of luncheon meats and cooked sausages with condiments and relishes can adapt themselves easily to many serving situations.

Arrange them casually and serve make-your-own-sandwiches with tall, cool beverages for a light supper at a summer get-together. Or, change the mood to elegance by using a fancy platter and a more formal table setting. Because you do the work ahead of time and each person helps himself, cold meat trays are equally suited to small or large numbers of guests.

In addition, luncheon meats and sausages coordinate well with many side dishes. Choose any of the following suggestions for side-dishes or substitute your own favorites: cottage cheese mixtures, potato or macaroni salads, baked beans, marinated bean or vegetable salads, tossed salads, molded gelatin salads with fruit or vegetables, vegetable soufflés and assorted cheeses. Hot and cold soups make nice appetizers or menu accompaniments for this type of meal — winter or summer.

COLD MEAT TRAY

   Minced Ham
   Bologna
   Chopped Cured Pork
   Salami
   Liver Sausage or
      Braunschweiger
   Liver Sausage and Cheese
   Head Cheese
   Jellied Veal Loaf
   Corned Beef Loaf
   Meat Loaf
   Cooked Ham
   Roast Beef

Cut large slices in half so each person can have some of each kind of meat. Arrange slices to make serving easy.

Place meat on tray in an attractive arrangement (flat slices, folded slices or rolled slices). Make cornucopias and fill with potato salad or cottage cheese. Garnish with parsley, radishes, olives, tomato wedges or slices, pickles or pickled fruits.

Hearty Beef Salad, opposite page

Meat salads

Salads are a versatile way to use "planned-over" meat. Leftovers used in meat salads can be an interesting accompaniment to a soup or sandwich supper — or they can be a meal in themselves.

Hearty main dish salads are easy make-aheads for the hostess. The salad can be prepared ahead of time, covered and refrigerated. Add juicy ingredients (such as tomatoes) or extra crisp ingredients (such as nuts) at the last minute, and arrange the salad greens just before serving. If the entire salad will not be eaten at one time, toss juicy and extra crisp ingredients with only the number of servings needed. The leftovers can be planned for another day.

Main dish salads can be served in large individual bowls or on plates. Serve each portion individually, or arrange all the ingredients in a large bowl and let each person serve himself. Colorful garnishes, such as carrot curls, radish slices or flowers, hard-cooked egg slices, pimiento strips, tomato wedges, cucumber slices, parsley or watercress make these salads elegant and even more appealing.

A fairly sweet but hearty beef salad. Leftovers shine when tossed with French dressing and mayonnaise. Note tip for using cubed potatoes.

HEARTY BEEF SALAD

    1 hard-cooked egg, cut into wedges
    2 cups cubed cooked beef
    ½ cup (1 med.) shredded carrot
    ½ cup prepared French or Russian dressing
    ⅓ cup mayonnaise or salad dressing
    1¾ cups (10-oz. pkg.) frozen peas, cooked and drained

3 TO 4 SERVINGS

In large mixing bowl, combine all ingredients except peas; mix well. Add peas; toss very lightly. Chill before serving. If desired, garnish with parsley.

Tips: For an extra hearty beef salad, add 1 medium potato, cooked and cubed, with the beef.

If desired, 1¾ cups (10-oz. pkg.) frozen peas and carrots can be used for the peas. Omit shredded carrot.

If desired, 1 cup (8-oz. can) drained peas can be used for the frozen peas.

Meat and potatoes in a salad — what a way to use leftovers! Dill pickle adds the tartness; celery the crisp crunch.

BEEF 'N TATER SALAD

    2 cups cubed cooked potatoes*
    3 cups cubed cooked beef
    1 medium stalk celery, chopped
    ¼ cup chopped dill pickle
    1 tablespoon chopped pimiento
    ½ teaspoon salt or seasoned salt
    ⅓ cup mayonnaise or salad dressing
    1 tablespoon pickle liquid

4 SERVINGS

In large mixing bowl, combine all ingredients; mix well. Chill before serving. If desired, garnish with chopped parsley.

Tip: *2 medium potatoes, cooked and cubed, will give the 2 cups needed for this recipe.

Use leftover beef in this salad — Cantonese style! Chow mein noodles add the crunchiness to this easy beef salad. Follow the tip for an extra hearty salad. They'll never know it's leftover beef.

CHOW BEEF SALAD

    2 hard-cooked eggs, chopped
    3 cups cubed cooked beef
    1 medium stalk celery, chopped
    ¼ cup sweet pickle relish or chopped sweet pickle
    ⅓ cup mayonnaise or salad dressing
    1 tablespoon Worcestershire sauce or soy sauce
    2½ cups (3-oz. can) chow mein noodles

4 TO 6 SERVINGS

In large mixing bowl, combine all ingredients except chow mein noodles; mix well. Just before serving, add chow mein noodles; toss lightly. If desired, garnish with mandarin oranges.

Tips: If desired, ½ cup (5-oz. can) drained and sliced water chestnuts can be added with the mayonnaise.

If an extra hearty salad is desired, 1 cup cooked rice and 1½ cups (10-oz. pkg.) cooked and drained frozen pea pods can be added with the chow mein noodles.

All the fixings for tacos but in a salad. A tasty, hearty salad that can be made ahead. Serve it warm in only 30 minutes. Great for a summer supper!

TACO SALAD

  1 lb. ground beef
  ½ cup (1 small) chopped onion or 2 tablespoons instant minced onion
  1 package (1¼ oz.) taco seasoning mix*
  ½ cup hot water
  ½ head lettuce, torn into pieces
  1 cup (6-oz. pkg.) corn chips
  ¾ cup (3 oz.) shredded Cheddar or American cheese
  2 medium tomatoes, cut in wedges

Dressing

  ⅓ cup chili sauce
  ¼ teaspoon hot pepper sauce

4 TO 6 SERVINGS

In large fry pan, brown meat and onion; drain excess fat. Stir in dry taco seasoning mix and water; simmer 10 minutes over low heat. Line separate salad bowls or plate with lettuce; sprinkle with corn chips. Mound about ½ cup beef mixture in center; sprinkle with cheese. Garnish with tomatoes. Serve immediately with Dressing or prepared French, Caesar or Russian dressing. Serve hot.

Dressing: Combine chili sauce and hot pepper sauce; mix well.

Tips: *If you don't have taco seasoning mix, add ½ cup chili sauce, 1 teaspoon salt, 1 teaspoon chili powder and ¼ teaspoon hot pepper sauce with water.

Beef mixture can be made ahead and reheated just before serving. If necessary, thin with additional water.

Corned beef and cabbage take on a new face in this salad. Especially easy using leftover carved beef or canned corned beef. Hearty enough for the hungry man of the house.

DILLY CORNED BEEF SALAD

  2 cups cubed cooked potato*
  ½ medium head cabbage, shredded or thinly sliced
  2 cups cubed cooked corned beef**
  ½ cup chopped dill pickle
  ¼ cup chopped onion or 1 tablespoon instant minced onion
  ¼ teaspoon salt
  ½ cup mayonnaise or salad dressing

5 TO 6 SERVINGS

In large mixing bowl, combine all ingredients; mix well. Chill before serving. Serve on lettuce. If desired, garnish with radish slices.

Tips: *2 medium potatoes, cooked and cubed, will give the 2 cups needed for this recipe.

**A 12-oz. can corned beef, cubed, contains the 2 cups needed for this recipe.

Cheese cubes and wiener slices are tossed together for an easy salad — a nice change from the regular meal routine.

CHEESE AND WIENER SALAD

  1 lb. wieners, cut into 1-inch slices
  2 cups (8 oz.) cubed mild Cheddar or American cheese
  3 tablespoons sweet pickle relish or chopped sweet pickle
  1 tablespoon chopped pimiento, if desired
  ⅓ cup mayonnaise or salad dressing

4 TO 5 SERVINGS

In large mixing bowl, combine all ingredients; mix well. Chill before serving. Serve on lettuce or cabbage leaves with celery or carrot sticks.

This traditional main dish salad can be a great way to use your leftover ham. Serve it with hot rolls and fruit for a refreshing meal! Pictured on page 14

CHEF'S SALAD

  3 hard-cooked eggs, sliced
  1 clove garlic, if desired
  2 heads lettuce, torn into bite-size pieces
  ½ teaspoon salt
    Dash pepper
  ½ cup sliced radishes
  1 to 2 cups cooked chicken, cut in strips
  1 to 2 cups cooked ham, cut in strips
  1 cup (4 oz.) Swiss or Cheddar cheese, cut in strips
  ½ cup mayonnaise or salad dressing

6 SERVINGS

If desired, rub salad bowl with cut clove of garlic; discard garlic. In salad bowl, toss lettuce with salt, pepper and sliced radishes. Arrange meat and cheese over lettuce. Top with sliced hard-cooked eggs. Serve with mayonnaise.

Tip: Any combination of salad greens can be used for the lettuce, such as fresh spinach leaves, watercress and parsley.

Traditional franks and kraut are tossed with macaroni and sweetened with a touch of brown sugar. Especially for those who are watching pennies!

SWEET-SOUR FRANK SALAD

  1 lb. wieners, cut into 1-inch slices
  2 cups cooked macaroni*
  1 cup (8-oz. can) drained sauerkraut
  1 to 2 tablespoons brown sugar

4 TO 5 SERVINGS

In large mixing bowl, combine all ingredients; mix well. Chill before serving. Serve on cabbage leaves. If desired, garnish with green pepper or cucumber slices.

Tip: *¾ cup uncooked macaroni will give the 2 cups cooked macaroni needed for this recipe.

HAM SALAD

2 hard-cooked eggs, chopped
3 cups cubed cooked ham
½ cup (1 med. stalk) chopped celery
½ cup sweet pickle relish or chopped sweet pickle
½ cup mayonnaise or salad dressing
2 teaspoons prepared mustard or ½ teaspoon dry mustard
Dash pepper

4 SERVINGS

In medium mixing bowl, combine all ingredients; mix well. Chill before serving. Serve in lettuce cups. If desired, garnish with tomato wedges.

Tips: If desired, 2 cups (12-oz. can) cubed luncheon meat can be used for the ham.

For a sweeter salad, 1 tablespoon pickle liquid can be added with the mustard.

HAM AND CHEESE SALAD

3 cups cubed cooked ham
1½ cups cooked macaroni*
1½ cups (8 oz.) cubed Swiss cheese
1 cup (2 med. stalks) chopped celery
2 tomatoes, cubed
1 tablespoon chopped parsley or parsley flakes
½ teaspoon salt
Dash pepper
½ cup prepared sour cream or bleu cheese dressing

6 TO 8 SERVINGS

In large mixing bowl, combine all ingredients, mix well. Chill before serving. Serve on lettuce leaves. If desired, garnish with crumbled bleu cheese.

Tip: *½ cup uncooked macaroni will give the 1½ cups cooked macaroni needed for this recipe.

SALAMI AND CHEESE SALAD

1 lb. salami, cubed
1 to 2 cups (4 to 8 oz.) cubed or shredded Cheddar or Swiss cheese
¼ cup chopped green pepper
2 tablespoons chopped chives or green onion
½ cup mayonnaise or salad dressing
1 cup croutons or herb seasoned bread stuffing

4 TO 6 SERVINGS

In large mixing bowl, combine all ingredients except croutons; mix well. Just before serving, add croutons; toss lightly. Serve on lettuce. If desired, garnish with tomato wedges.

Tips: If desired, prepared Caesar salad dressing can be used for the mayonnaise. Omit cheese.

For Bologna and Cheese Salad, 1 lb. cubed bologna can be used for the salami.

Salami and Cheese Salad, above

Gravies, sauces and marinades

The flavor and texture of gravies and sauces can add a special touch to many types of meat. Roasts become gourmet accomplishments; leftovers look like new; chops and steaks take on an elegant air; and ground meat patties seem extra special. The introductory Tips will give you suggestions on which types of meats are especially enhanced by the particular sauce or gravy. Branch out and vary your repertoire of recipes with some of these exciting sauces.

Marinades, too, add subtle flavors and new interest to favorite meat cuts. Flavors blend and permeate the meat while marinating, adding flavor and tenderness. Longer marinating times, of course, give more flavor than shorter marinating times. Drain the marinade before cooking the meat, and store it covered, in the refrigerator so it can be used another time.

ROASTING PAN GRAVY

    2 cups liquid
    ¼ cup meat drippings
    ¼ cup flour
    ½ cup cold liquid
    Salt to taste
    Pepper to taste

2½ CUPS SAUCE

Add liquid to drippings in roasting pan. Combine flour and cold liquid. Blend until smooth. Add flour mixture to hot liquid, stirring constantly. Cook until mixture thickens and comes to a boil. Season with salt and pepper. Serve hot.

Tip: For interesting flavor, use seasoned salt for the salt.

SKILLET GRAVY

    3 tablespoons meat drippings
    3 tablespoons flour
    2 cups liquid
    Salt to taste
    Pepper to taste

2 CUPS SAUCE

Shake or spoon flour into drippings in skillet. Blend over low heat until smooth and browned. Gradually add liquid. Cook, stirring constantly, until mixture thickens. Season with salt and pepper.

Tips: Flour and drippings can be decreased to 2 tablespoons for thin gravy; increased to 4 tablespoons for thick gravy.

For Milk Gravy, use 2 cups milk for liquid.

BROWN SAUCE

    2 tablespoons butter or
      margarine
    2 tablespoons flour
    2 cups hot water
    2 beef bouillon cubes or
      2 teaspoons instant bouillon
    ½ teaspoon salt
    ⅛ teaspoon pepper

2 CUPS SAUCE

Melt butter in saucepan. Add flour and cook until golden brown. Add bouillon cubes and gradually the hot water. Cook, stirring constantly, until mixture thickens and comes to a boil.

Tip: If desired, 1⅓ cups (10½-oz. can) condensed beef bouillon or beef consommé can be used with water to make 2 cups liquid.

BORDELAISE SAUCE

    2 cups (1 recipe) Brown
      Sauce
    2 tablespoons minced green
      onion
    1 clove garlic
    1 carrot, finely chopped
    1 small bay leaf
    4 peppercorns
    ½ teaspoon chopped parsley,
      if desired
    Dash ground thyme, if
      desired

2½ CUPS SAUCE

Prepare Brown Sauce as directed, sautéing onion, garlic, carrot, bay leaf and peppercorns in butter before adding flour. Strain to remove vegetables before serving. Add parsley and thyme. Serve warm.

BASIC WHITE SAUCE

    ¼ cup butter or margarine
    ¼ cup flour
    2 cups milk
    ½ teaspoon salt
    ⅛ teaspoon pepper

2 CUPS SAUCE

Melt butter in saucepan over low heat. Blend in flour. Gradually add milk. Cook, stirring constantly, until mixture thickens and comes to a boil. Season with salt and pepper. If necessary, sauce can be covered and kept over hot (but not boiling) water until serving time.

Rich White Sauce
Prepare Basic White Sauce. Blend ⅓ cup light cream with 1 egg yolk; then add to heated sauce. Cook, stirring constantly, until thick. Makes 2½ cups sauce.

Nippy Cheese Sauce
Prepare Basic White Sauce, decreasing butter and flour to 3 tablespoons each. Add 2 cups (8 oz.) shredded Cheddar cheese, 2 teaspoons Worcestershire sauce, dash Tabasco sauce and dash cayenne pepper. Makes 3 cups sauce.

Cheese-Dill Sauce
Prepare Basic White Sauce. Add to heated sauce ⅓ cup shredded Cheddar cheese, 2 tablespoons crushed dill seed. Heat until cheese melts. Makes 2½ cups sauce.

Pimiento Cheese Sauce
Prepare Basic White Sauce, sautéing 3 tablespoons green pepper in the melted butter before adding flour. When white sauce is thickened, add 1½ cups (6 oz.) shredded Cheddar cheese, ⅓ cup canned sliced mushrooms and 2 tablespoons chopped pimiento. Continue cooking until cheese melts. Makes 3 cups sauce.

VELOUTÉ SAUCE

¼ cup butter or margarine, melted
¼ cup flour
½ teaspoon salt
1½ cups chicken or veal broth*
½ cup light cream or milk

2 CUPS SAUCE

Melt butter in saucepan over low heat. Blend in flour and salt until smooth. Add broth and cream. Cook, stirring constantly, until mixture thickens and comes to a boil. If necessary, sauce can be covered and kept over hot (but not boiling) water until serving time.

Tip: *If desired, 1½ cups water and 2 chicken bouillon cubes or 2 teaspoons instant bouillon can be used for the chicken broth.

A few additions to a Velouté Sauce make it a good partner for ham, as well as veal and lamb.

BÉCHAMEL SAUCE

2 cups (1 recipe) Velouté Sauce
1 teaspoon instant minced onion
Dash nutmeg
Dash thyme

2 CUPS SAUCE

Combine all ingredients; mix well. Serve hot, immediately.

Ideal for serving with leftovers or as a dressing for a meaty salad. Corned beef, beef and ham are especially suited to this flavor.

HORSERADISH SAUCE

1 cup dairy sour cream
2 tablespoons cream-style horseradish
2 tablespoons finely-chopped dill pickle
½ teaspoon salt
⅛ teaspoon paprika

1 CUP SAUCE

Combine ingredients. Chill and serve.

SOUR CREAM SAUCE

1 cup dairy sour cream
2 tablespoons cooking oil
1 tablespoon lemon juice
½ teaspoon salt
½ teaspoon curry powder
⅛ teaspoon pepper

1 CUP SAUCE

In small saucepan, combine all ingredients. Bring just to boiling point, but do not boil. Serve immediately.

Swiss and American cheeses combine to add an excitingly different flavor to this creamy sauce. Great with veal, pork or lamb.

MORNAY SAUCE

¾ cup boiling water
¼ cup butter or margarine
1 chicken bouillon cube or
1 teaspoon instant bouillon
¼ cup flour
¾ cup light cream
½ cup grated Parmesan cheese
½ cup shredded Swiss cheese

3 CUPS SAUCE

In saucepan, combine water, butter and bouillon cube. Heat over medium heat until butter is melted and cube is dissolved. Blend in flour; add cream. Cook, stirring constantly, until thick. Blend in bouillon and cheeses. Stir until smooth. Serve hot.

Canned soup makes a convenient base for a speedy cheese sauce. Great with any meat.

QUICK AND EASY CHEESE SAUCE

1⅓ cups (10½-oz. can) condensed cream of mushroom soup
⅓ cup milk
½ cup shredded American cheese

1¾ CUPS SAUCE

In saucepan, combine soup and milk. Heat until bubbly; reduce heat. Add cheese; stir until melted.

CREAMY MUSTARD SAUCE

1 egg, separated
1 cup light cream or milk
1 teaspoon flour
¼ cup sugar
2 tablespoons dry mustard
½ teaspoon salt
⅛ teaspoon pepper
2 tablespoons vinegar

2 CUPS SAUCE

Beat egg yolk in small saucepan. Add cream, flour, sugar, mustard, salt and pepper. Blend until smooth. Cook over medium heat, stirring constantly, until mixture thickens and comes to a boil. Stir in vinegar. Beat egg white until stiff and fold into sauce. Serve warm.

Use your blender to whip up this tangy sauce — great over beef or veal.

QUICK HOLLANDAISE SAUCE (Blender)

2 egg yolks
1 tablespoon lemon juice
¼ teaspoon salt
Dash cayenne pepper
½ cup butter or margarine

¾ CUP SAUCE

Combine egg yolks, lemon juice, salt and cayenne pepper in blender. Heat butter until bubbly but not brown. While processing egg mixture on medium speed, pour melted butter slowly into blender. Blend just until thick. Serve immediately.

HERB LEMON SAUCE

½ cup cooking oil
¼ cup lemon juice
1 teaspoon instant minced onion
1 teaspoon salt
¼ teaspoon ground thyme
⅛ teaspoon ground marjoram
Dash pepper
2 cloves garlic, crushed

¾ CUP SAUCE

Combine all ingredients in a mixing bowl; mix well. Store, covered, in refrigerator after using.

CREAMY MUSHROOM SAUCE

- 1½ cups (8 oz. or ½ lb.) sliced fresh mushrooms
- ¼ cup butter or margarine
- ¼ cup flour
- 1⅓ cups (10-oz. can) condensed beef or chicken bouillon
- ½ cup light cream
- ¼ teaspoon salt
- 2 tablespoons chopped parsley
- Dash pepper

3 CUPS SAUCE

In saucepan, sauté mushrooms in butter until golden. Cover; let simmer 5 minutes. Blend in ¼ cup flour. Add beef broth slowly, stirring until smooth. Stir in cream, salt, parsley and pepper. Heat just until mixture simmers.

Tip: If desired, ½ cup (4-oz. can) drained mushrooms can be used for the fresh. Omit salt.

MUSHROOM SAUCE

- ¼ cup butter or margarine
- 1½ cups (8 oz. or 1 lb.) sliced fresh mushrooms
- 1 cup water
- 2 teaspoons cornstarch
- 1 teaspoon salt
- 1 teaspoon Worcestershire sauce
- Dash pepper

1½ CUPS SAUCE

Melt butter in saucepan. Sauté mushrooms in butter until tender. Combine water and cornstarch. Blend into hot mushrooms, stirring constantly, until mixture thickens and comes to a boil. Add Worcestershire sauce and seasonings. Serve hot.

CUMBERLAND SAUCE

- 1 cup (10-oz. jar) currant jelly
- ½ teaspoon dry mustard
- 1 tablespoon grated orange rind
- 1 tablespoon grated lemon rind
- ¼ cup orange juice
- 1 tablespoon lemon juice
- ⅛ teaspoon ground ginger

1 CUP SAUCE

Combine ingredients in saucepan. Heat, stirring occasionally, until jelly melts. Cook until mixture is smooth. Serve hot.

SWEET-SOUR SAUCE

- ½ cup pineapple juice
- 2 tablespoons vinegar
- 2 tablespoons brown sugar
- ⅛ teaspoon pepper
- ½ teaspoon paprika
- 1 chicken bouillon cube or 1 teaspoon instant bouillon
- ½ teaspoon prepared mustard
- 1 tablespoon cornstarch
- ¼ cup water

1 CUP SAUCE

In small saucepan, combine all ingredients except cornstarch and water. Cook until bouillon cube is dissolved. Combine cornstarch and water. Stir into hot liquid. Cook, stirring constantly, until mixture thickens and comes to a boil.

SPICY RAISIN SAUCE

- ½ cup firmly packed brown sugar
- 1 tablespoon cornstarch
- 1½ teaspoons dry mustard
- ⅛ teaspoon ground cloves
- 1 cup water
- 2 tablespoons lemon juice
- ¼ cup raisins
- 1 tablespoon butter or margarine

1 CUP SAUCE

Combine sugar, cornstarch, mustard and cloves. Blend in lemon juice and water; stir until smooth. Cook, stirring constantly, until clear and thick. Add raisins and butter. Cook about 10 minutes to plump raisins. Serve hot.

CHERRY-ORANGE SAUCE

- 2 cups (1-lb. can) pitted sour red cherries, reserve liquid
- ¼ cup sugar
- 2 tablespoons cornstarch
- 1 cup orange juice
- 1 tablespoon lemon juice
- Reserved 1 cup cherry liquid
- 2 teaspoons grated orange rind, if desired
- ½ stick cinnamon or ⅛ teaspoon ground cinnamon
- ½ teaspoon whole cloves or ⅛ teaspoon ground cloves
- Dash salt
- ⅛ to ¼ teaspoon red food coloring, if desired

3 CUPS SAUCE

Drain cherries; reserve syrup, adding water to make 1 cup liquid. In medium saucepan, combine all ingredients, except cherries. Cook, stirring constantly, over medium heat until mixture thickens and comes to a boil. Stir in cherries. Serve hot.

Tip: Frozen cherries can be used for the canned cherries. If no cherry liquid is available, orange juice or water can be used.

This tangy sauce has an especially good flavor and makes these hamburgers a special feature on our take-along picnic. Shape the patties ahead of time and take along your grill (ours is a hibachi) to cook them.
We served Baked Beans and Potato Salad (which were made ahead and taken in containers with tight-fitting covers) to help round out the meal.

BARBECUE SAUCE SPECIAL

3 tablespoons sugar
2 tablespoons flour or cornstarch
2 teaspoons salt or seasoned salt
1 cup water
1 cup (8-oz. can) tomato sauce
½ cup (1 med.) chopped onion or 2 tablespoons instant minced onion
3 tablespoons Worcestershire sauce
2 tablespoons prepared mustard

2 CUPS SAUCE

In small saucepan, combine all ingredients; mix well. Cook, stirring constantly, over medium heat until mixture thickens and comes to a boil. Use on any meat for broiling or barbecuing. Or, cool and store, covered, in refrigerator for later use.

SPEEDY BARBECUE SAUCE

1 package (⅝ oz.) Pillsbury Brown Gravy Mix
1 cup cold water
1 cup catsup
1 tablespoon prepared mustard
½ teaspoon Worcestershire sauce

2 CUPS SAUCE

Combine gravy mix and cold water. Add catsup, mustard and Worcestershire sauce. Cook over low heat, stirring constantly, until mixture thickens and comes to a boil.

EASY BARBECUE SAUCE

1 cup (8-oz. can) tomato sauce
¼ cup prepared barbecue sauce
1 tablespoon instant minced onion
1 lemon, thinly sliced
2 tablespoons brown sugar
1 teaspoon garlic salt
½ teaspoon dry mustard
⅛ teaspoon pepper

1½ CUPS SAUCE

Combine all ingredients; mix well. Let stand 15 to 20 minutes to blend flavors. Store, covered, in refrigerator after using.

QUICK AND EASY TOMATO SAUCE

1 cup (8-oz. can) tomato sauce
½ cup water
1 teaspoon Worcestershire sauce
½ teaspoon salt
Dash pepper

1½ CUPS SAUCE

Combine ingredients in saucepan. Heat and serve.

TOMATO-MUSHROOM SAUCE

2 cloves garlic, crushed
2 tablespoons cooking oil
1 cup (8-oz. can) drained sliced mushrooms
2 cups (1-lb. can) undrained tomatoes
1 cup (8-oz. can) tomato sauce
¾ cup (6-oz. can) tomato paste
1 tablespoon sugar
1 teaspoon salt
1 teaspoon crushed basil
Dash cayenne pepper

4 CUPS SAUCE

Sauté garlic in oil in frypan until golden. Add mushrooms and sauté 10 minutes. Stir in remaining ingredients. Simmer, uncovered, 1 hour until flavors are well blended. This marinade can be drained after using and stored, covered, in refrigerator for reuse.

ZESTY BARBECUE SAUCE

½ cup (1 med.) chopped onion or 2 tablespoons instant minced onion
1 clove garlic, crushed
¼ cup cooking oil
1 cup catsup
½ cup water
¼ cup firmly packed brown sugar
3 tablespoons Worcestershire sauce
2 teaspoons prepared mustard
1 teaspoon salt
¼ teaspoon ground thyme
1 lemon, thinly sliced
Dash Tabasco sauce

2½ CUPS SAUCE

Sauté onion and garlic in oil in saucepan until tender. Add remaining ingredients; mix well. Bring to a boil and simmer for 5 minutes. Store, covered, in refrigerator after using.

WHITE WINE VINEGAR MARINADE

½ cup olive or cooking oil
½ cup white wine vinegar
1 medium onion, chopped or 2 tablespoons instant minced onion
2 cloves garlic, crushed

1⅓ CUPS MARINADE

Combine all ingredients, mix well. This marinade can be drained after using and stored, covered, in refrigerator for reuse.

SPEEDY SAUCE MARINADE

1 package (7/10 oz.) Italian salad dressing mix
½ cup water
½ cup catsup
1 teaspoon prepared mustard
¼ teaspoon Worcestershire sauce

1¼ CUPS MARINADE

Combine all ingredients; mix well. This marinade can be drained after using and stored, covered, in refrigerator for reuse.

BEEF TERIYAKI MARINADE

1 cup soy sauce
¼ cup sugar
2 tablespoons finely chopped onion or 2 teaspoons instant minced onion
1¼ teaspoons ground ginger
4 bay leaves, crushed
4 cloves garlic, crushed

1⅓ CUPS MARINADE

Combine all ingredients; stir until blended. This marinade can be drained after using and stored, covered, in refrigerator for reuse.

PORK TERIYAKI MARINADE

1½ cups soy sauce
¾ cup honey
1½ teaspoons ground ginger
¼ teaspoon ground thyme
1 clove garlic, crushed

2¼ CUPS MARINADE

Combine all ingredients; mix well. This marinade can be drained after using and stored, covered, in refrigerator for reuse.

Outdoor cooking

Barbecued Ribs, opposite page

Cook tonight's dinner outside; Barbecued Spareribs are ideal for your next patio dinner. We've served a Crisp Tossed Salad, Skewered Acorn Squash and Rice Pilaf with Mushrooms at this barbecue.

124

Barbecuing has become a favorite all across America. Not only is summer barbecuing a pastime for many families, but indoor barbecues now extend this enjoyment into the winter months.

The mouth-watering aroma of charcoal broiled or roasted meat has appealed for many years to both old and young. Originally, the entire animal was roasted on a spit over an open fire. From this, the tradition of roasting over coals (or barbecuing) has been adapted. Picnics, campfires, fireplaces — what a variety of occasions to get into the outdoor spirit!

Any of the tender cuts of meat are suitable for barbecuing. In addition, the less tender cuts can be tenderized or precooked and also adapted for cooking-on-the-grill. Roasts, ribs, tender steaks, weiners, hamburger or sausage, ham or bacon, and kabob combinations are some of the choices which are available. Combine these with cold salads, crisp relishes, foil-roasted vegetables, bread or pie warmed on the grill, and hot or cold beverages for a colorful and flavorful zip to outdoor meals.

Whether your equipment is as simple as a foil-lined hole in the ground with a metal grill, or the most elaborate electric-powered rotisserie, you can get the most from your equipment by following a few basic guidelines for fire building and barbecue cookery.

THE FIRE

Line the fire bowl with heavy-duty foil for easiest cleaning. A one-inch layer of gravel, cinders, sand, or small rocks in the bottom of the fire bowl permits the fire to "breathe" and will give more heat from the coals.
Make a pile of 12 to 15 briquettes when using chemical fire starters. Soak the briquettes with charcoal lighter fluid and let stand several minutes before lighting, so that the starter penetrates the briquettes. (Lump charcoal ignites more quickly; it is less expensive, burns

faster and has more charcoal aroma. Briquettes provide longer, hotter heat.)

When the briquettes are covered with gray ash, spread the coals evenly over the cooking area. Your fire is ready! (If you use wood, avoid wood that gives an objectionable odor or flavor to food. Cooking times may be slightly altered, depending on the intensity of heat from your fire.)

Start the fire from 30 to 35 minutes before you plan to begin cooking. In order to keep a fire burning, it must have adequate ventilation. Some units have a damper to control the flow of air around the fire. Grills which have no air vents in the firebox should be placed so that natural breezes will help to ventilate the coals. Too much air tends to make the coals burn too quickly — making your heat less efficient — whereas, too little air will tend to retard their burning and sometimes gives insufficient heat.

THE GRILL

Briquettes should be spread evenly, about one-inch apart, over the cooking area. Rub the grill with fat or cooking oil to prevent meat from sticking to the rack. Adjust the height of the rack, measuring from the top of the coals. Trim excess fat from meat to prevent flaming and excess smoking.

THE ROTISSERIE

Arrange the lighted briquettes at the rear of the fire bowl. For even, moderate cooking temperature, start with a small amount of charcoal and add more as needed. Control the amount of heat by adjusting the height of the grill or the fire box, or by adding or removing briquettes. Consult your operating manual for instructions on threading the skewer so that the weight is balanced and cooking is even.

Corn on the cob, French bread and barbecued ribs make for a favorite cook-out. These are especially easy on the chef because they're pre-cooked and then grilled for about 20 minutes.

BARBECUED RIBS

4 to 4½ lbs. country-style ribs or spareribs, cut into serving pieces

Barbecue Sauce
½ cup catsup
½ cup chili sauce or tomato sauce
2 tablespoons brown sugar
¼ cup (1 small) chopped onion
1 teaspoon celery seed, if desired
½ teaspoon salt
⅛ teaspoon instant minced garlic or garlic powder or 1 clove garlic, minced
2 teaspoons prepared or dry mustard
1 tablespoon Worcestershire sauce
Dash Tabasco sauce
½ lemon, sliced or 1 tablespoon lemon juice

6 TO 8 SERVINGS

In large saucepan, cover ribs with water; salt to taste. Simmer, covered, over medium low heat for 1 hour; (meanwhile prepare Barbecue Sauce). Drain ribs; place in covered dish. Pour Barbecue Sauce over, coating each rib. Let cool*; cover and refrigerate overnight. Grill over hot coals or broil until browned and heated through, about 20 minutes, brushing with sauce as necessary.

Barbecue Sauce: Combine all ingredients; mix well.

Tips: *By refrigerating the ribs in the sauce, there is more time for the flavors to penetrate into the meat; however they can be grilled immediately by brushing with the sauce during cooking.

For an easier Barbecue Sauce, use 1 cup prepared barbecue sauce along with onion, celery seed, garlic, mustard and lemon.

HANDY EQUIPMENT

Gloves — Canvas or asbestos gloves are ideal for handling fuel, adjusting or moving the grill, spreading fire or handling hot pots and pans.

Tongs — Long handled tongs are best for turning steaks, lifting pots and pans, etc., because the chef's hands are further away from the intense heat.

Basting brush — A long-handled pastry brush or paint brush is handy for spreading sauces over foods while they are grilling.

Skewers — Metal skewers with one sharp end come in a variety of lengths, especially suited to the particular type of kabobs you're planning.

Other useful items — Long-handled salt and pepper shakers are handy and convenient. Keep towels, paper towels, and pot holders nearby for any spills or special uses by the chef.

Teriyaki flavored pork chops cooked well done on a barbecue! Allow to marinate 2 hours for full-bodied flavor. (Or, marinate for a shorter time for a milder flavor.) We've served ours (see photo) with Baked Potatoes, Corn on the Cob, Marinated Bean Salad and Fresh Fruit.

KOREAN BARBECUED PORK CHOPS

½ cup soy sauce
½ cup dry sherry
2 tablespoons sesame seeds, if desired
1 tablespoon dry mustard
1 teaspoon ground ginger
½ teaspoon minced garlic
6 to 10 pork chops

6 TO 10 SERVINGS

In shallow pan or plastic bag, combine all ingredients except pork chops. Mix well; add chops. Marinate for ½ to 2 hours. Remove meat from marinade. (Marinade can be reserved for reuse.) Cook chops on grill or broil 3 to 4-inches from heat for 10 minutes on each side until done.

This economical cut of meat is right at home on the barbecue and will be a treat for your family. It is flavored with a marinade and needs only potato salad and coleslaw to turn it into a royal barbecue supper!

MARINATED MINUTE STEAKS

¾ cup cooking oil
¼ cup soy sauce
3 tablespoons honey
2 tablespoons vinegar
1 to 2 tablespoons chopped green onion
1½ teaspoons ground ginger
⅛ teaspoon garlic powder
6 minute steaks

6 SERVINGS

Combine all ingredients except steaks in plastic bag or shallow pan. Add steaks. Let stand 1 to 2 hours. Grill 4 to 5 inches from hot coals for 5 to 7 minutes on each side, brushing frequently with marinade.

Flank steak becomes tender and flavorful as it marinates in this teriyaki marinade. Serve with rice, buttered green beans and a fruit salad.

TERIYAKI STEAK

½ cup (5-oz. bottle) soy sauce
1 clove garlic, minced or ⅛ teaspoon instant minced garlic
2 tablespoons brown sugar
½ teaspoon ground ginger
2 tablespoons Worcestershire sauce
1 tablespoon lemon juice
1 flank steak (1½ to 2 lbs.)

4 TO 6 SERVINGS

In shallow bowl or plastic bag, combine all ingredients except flank steak. Add steak, coating with marinade. Cover tightly and refrigerate 6 to 24 hours, turning occasionally. Remove from marinade. Broil or grill over hot coals, placing about 2 inches from heat and broiling about 5 minutes on each side. To serve, cut across the grain into thin slices.

Tip: For 2 servings, halve all ingredients. Prepare as directed. Remaining half of Flank Steak can be frozen or used later in another recipe, such as London Broil, page 35.

A flavorful way to prepare a less tender steak for barbecuing. Serve with crusty French bread, potato salad and a relish tray.

BARBECUED FAMILY STEAK

2 to 2½ lbs. family steak, sirloin tip steak or top round steak
Meat tenderizer
½ cup dry red wine
¼ cup cooking oil
1 tablespoon Worcestershire sauce
1 clove garlic, minced or ⅛ teaspoon instant minced garlic or garlic powder
1 small onion, chopped or 1 tablespoon instant minced onion

6 TO 8 SERVINGS

Prepare steak with tenderizer as directed on label. Place in plastic bag in shallow bowl. Combine remaining ingredients; pour over steak. Close tightly. Refrigerate to marinate, 12 to 24 hours, turning occasionally. Remove steak from marinade; with paper towel, remove excess moisture. Grill over hot coals until rare to medium rare. To serve, cut meat across grain into thin slices.

Tip: If desired, broil steak in oven, 3 to 4 inches from heat, depending on thickness.

For 3 to 4 servings, halve all ingredients. Prepare as directed.

Turn meat with tongs when broiling; piercing with a fork allows flavorful juices to escape.

To allow meat to turn freely on the spit, select fairly symmetrical cuts. Precooking meats is sometimes desirable. (Precooking Spareribs and Corned Beef shortens the cooking time.)

When cooking meat inside foil wrapping over grill, use heavy duty foil or a double thickness of regular weight. Wrap securely and leave room for expansion of air and moisture during cooking.

Korean Barbecued Pork Chops, opposite page

Start this boneless pork roast on the rotisserie 4 hours before you plan to serve. Serve with corn on the cob, potato salad and a fruit salad.

BARBECUED PORK LOIN

8 lbs. boneless pork
　loin roast
Salt
Pepper

Barbecue Sauce

½ cup (1 med.) chopped
　onion
1 clove garlic, minced or
　⅛ teaspoon instant minced
　garlic
2 tablespoons oil or
　shortening
1 cup catsup
½ cup water
¼ cup firmly packed brown
　sugar
1 teaspoon salt
¼ teaspoon crushed leaf
　thyme
3 tablespoons
　Worcestershire sauce
2 teaspoons prepared
　mustard
1 lemon, thinly sliced
Dash Tabasco sauce

　　　　12 TO 16 SERVINGS

Sprinkle meat with salt and pepper. Run spit through center of meat, making sure it is evenly balanced. Secure to rotisserie with heavy cord. Insert meat thermometer so tip is in center of roast but not resting in fat or on rod. Grill over hot coals for 2 hours until meat thermometer reaches 140°. Continue grilling, brushing with Barbecue Sauce every 20 minutes, until roast reaches 170° internal temperature, about 1½ to 2 hours longer.

Barbecue Sauce: Sauté onion and garlic in oil in fry pan until tender. Add remaining ingredients. Bring to a boil and simmer for 5 minutes.

Easy to do — and flavorful, too! Serve it with corn on the cob, baked potatoes and a crisp salad — live it up!

SIRLOIN STEAK WITH ROQUEFORT

¼ cup butter or margarine
¼ cup (2 oz.) Roquefort or
　blue cheese
Salt
Dash pepper
2 lbs. sirloin steak, cut
　1½-inches thick

　　　　　6 TO 8 SERVINGS

In small bowl, cream all ingredients, except steak. Trim excess fat from steak. Slash fat edge to prevent curling. Place steak on rack 6 inches above hot coals. Grill 10 to 15 minutes; turn. Spread with cheese mixture and grill 15 minutes longer for medium steak or until of desired doneness.

Going on a camp out, picnic, or just eating outside? Have an inexpensive but delicious barbecue with these burgers. Serve potato chips and the other favorites with them, too.

BEEF BURGERS RANCHERO

1 lb. ground beef
1 teaspoon salt
⅛ teaspoon pepper
½ cup chili sauce
2 tablespoons sliced stuffed
　green olives
1 teaspoon instant minced
　onion
1 teaspoon chili powder
4 hamburger buns

　　　　　　　4 SERVINGS

In large bowl, combine beef, salt and pepper; blend well. Shape into 4 patties. Place patties on rack, 6 inches above hot coals. Grill on both sides until browned and of desired doneness. Combine remaining ingredients except buns in a small saucepan. Bring just to boil. Serve sauce over meat on buns.

Use any flavor of wine to marinate this less tender cut of meat before grilling. It will be more tender if cooked to medium doneness. Start cooking foil-wrapped potatoes and corn on the cob ahead of time so they will finish cooking when the steak is done.

FAMILY STEAK GRILL

1½ to 2 lbs. family steak, cut
　1½ to 2-inches thick
Meat tenderizer
⅔ cup wine*
⅓ cup cooking oil

　　　　　6 TO 8 SERVINGS

Prepare meat with tenderizer according to directions on package. In shallow pan or plastic bag, combine meat, wine and oil. Refrigerate, covered, overnight (12 to 24 hrs.) Remove meat from marinade. Broil over grill or in broiler 4 to 5 inches from heat about 10 minutes on each side until of desired doneness.

Tip: *We particularly like the flavors which white or rosé wines give this steak. Try these or your favorites.

Marinate this less tender steak to increase its tenderness. The longer you marinate it, the more tender it will be.

HERB CHARCOAL STEAK

¾ cup lemon juice
½ cup chopped onion or
　2 tablespoons instant
　minced onion
¼ cup cooking oil
½ teaspoon salt
½ teaspoon celery salt,
　if desired
½ teaspoon onion salt
½ teaspoon leaf thyme,
　if desired
½ teaspoon leaf rosemary
½ teaspoon leaf oregano,
　if desired
2 cloves garlic, crushed
3 lbs. round steak, cut
　1½-inches thick

　　　　　6 TO 8 SERVINGS

In plastic bag or large shallow bowl, combine all ingredients except meat. Add meat and marinate 6 to 8 hours. Place steak on rack 6 inches above hot coals. Grill 10 to 15 minutes, basting occasionally. Turn, continue basting, and grill 10 to 15 minutes longer for medium done steak.

Herb Charcoal Steak, opposite page

Beef Kabobs, opposite page

BOLOGNA KABOBS

1 bologna ring (1 lb.), cut into
  1-inch pieces
6 to 8 (15-oz. can) drained
  whole potatoes
Apricot halves
Sweet pickle halves or
  slices
Whole pitted ripe olives

6 SERVINGS

On 6 skewers, alternate bologna, potatoes, apricot halves, pickles and olives — beginning and ending with bologna. Place on rack over hot coals and grill 3 to 4 inches from heat for 10 minutes on each side until bologna browns.

Tips: If desired, 2 packages (8 oz. each) brown and serve sausages, cut in half, can be used for the bologna.

Kabobs can be broiled in oven 3 to 4 inches from heat for 7 to 10 minutes on each side.

BEEF KABOBS

3 carrots, cut into 1-inch
  pieces
1 pint (8-oz.) cherry
  tomatoes
2 large green peppers
1 cup (8-oz. can) drained
  small whole onions
1⅓ cups (1 recipe) Beef
  Teriyaki Marinade
  (page 123)
1 lb. round steak, cut into
  1-inch cubes

6 SERVINGS

Cook carrot pieces in boiling salted water just until tender. Wash tomatoes and green pepper. Cut green pepper into 1-inch pieces. Marinate all ingredients in Marinade for 1 hour. Alternate ingredients on 6 skewers beginning and ending with beef. Place on rack over hot coals and

grill 3 to 4 inches from heat for 15 to 20 minutes on each side, basting frequently with marinade, until beef is well browned.

HAM KABOBS

1 lb. smoked cooked ham,
  cut into 1-inch cubes
Pineapple chunks
Apricot halves
1 cup (1 recipe) Sweet-Sour
  Sauce (page 121)

6 SERVINGS

On 6 skewers, alternate ham, pineapple and apricots. Brush with Sauce. Broil or place on rack over hot coals and grill 3 to 4 inches from heat for 15 to 20 minutes, turning occasionally and brushing with remaining Sauce during grilling.

WIENER-PINEAPPLE BROIL

1½ lbs. (12) wieners
3 tablespoons chili sauce
2 teaspoons prepared
  mustard
1 tablespoon brown sugar
1⅔ cups (1-lb. can) drained
  pineapple spears
12 slices bacon

BROIL   6 SERVINGS

Cut lengthwise slits almost through wieners. Combine chili sauce, mustard and brown sugar; mix well. Spread on cut surface of wieners. Insert 1 pineapple spear in each. Wrap with slice of bacon and fasten with wooden picks. Place on broiler rack. Broil 3 inches from heat 5 minutes, until lightly browned. Turn and broil 5 minutes longer, until bacon is done.

Tip: To make Wiener Birds, use strips of cheese for the pineapple spears.

BROWN AND SERVE SAUSAGE KABOBS

3 oranges
1 pint (8 oz. or ½ lb.) fresh
  mushrooms
1 large green pepper
12 small potatoes
2 packages (8 oz. each)
  brown and serve sausages

6 SERVINGS

Peel and quarter oranges. Wash mushrooms and green pepper. Cut green pepper into 1-inch pieces. Alternate oranges, potatoes, mushrooms, green pepper and sausage links on 6 skewers, beginning and ending with sausage. Place on rack over hot coals and grill 3 to 4 inches from heat for 15 minutes on each side until sausage browns. Serve hot.

WIENER KABOBS

1½ lbs. (12) wieners
¼ lb. (4 oz.) American cheese
12 slices bacon, cut in half
1¼ cups (1 recipe) Speedy
  Sauce Marinade (page 123)
4 stalks celery, cut into
  1-inch pieces
1 cup drained canned
  pineapple chunks

6 SERVINGS

Cut frankfurters in half lengthwise. Cut 12 slices of cheese the length and width of wieners. Place between wiener halves. Cut each in half crosswise. Wrap each wiener with half slice of bacon; fasten with a wooden pick. Marinate stuffed wieners, celery and pineapple in Marinade for 1 hour. Alternate wieners, pineapple and celery on 6 skewers, beginning and ending with wieners. Place on rack over hot coals and grill 3 to 4 inches from heat for 10 to 15 minutes on each side until bacon browns.

LEMON BARBECUED CHUCK STEAK

2½ to 3 lbs. chuck steak, cut 1½-inches thick
⅓ cup lemon juice
⅓ cup cooking oil
1 teaspoon MSG (mono-sodium glutamate), if desired
1 teaspoon instant minced onion or ¼ cup chopped onion
1 teaspoon salt
1 teaspoon grated lemon peel
2 teaspoons Worcestershire sauce
1 teaspoon prepared mustard
⅛ teaspoon pepper

4 TO 6 SERVINGS

Slash fat edges of meat. Place in shallow dish. Combine remaining ingredients; pour over steak. Let stand 3 hours at room temperature or overnight in refrigerator, turning several times. Remove steak from marinade. Grill over hot coals or broil 3 to 4 inches from heat until rare or medium, brushing on marinade during cooking. To serve, cut into thin slices, across grain.

LONDON MARINATED ROUND STEAK

1½ lbs. round steak
Meat tenderizer
1 clove garlic, sliced
½ cup cooking oil
½ cup vinegar
1 teaspoon salt
¼ teaspoon pepper
2 teaspoons dry mustard
2 teaspoons Worcestershire sauce
Dash cayenne pepper
Few drops Tabasco sauce

4 TO 6 SERVINGS

Prepare round steak with meat tenderizer as directed on package. Combine with remaining ingredients in shallow pan or plastic bag. Let stand in refrigerator 12 hours or overnight. Remove meat from marinade. Broil 3 inches from heat for 4 to 7 minutes on each side for 1-inch steak or 8 to 12 minutes on each side for 2-inch steak. Carve diagonally across grain into thin slices.

BUDGET STEAK

3 lbs. round steak, cut 2-inches thick
Meat tenderizer
1 cup water
¼ cup soy sauce
¼ cup firmly packed brown sugar
¼ cup lemon juice
1 tablespoon Worcestershire sauce
1 tablespoon minced parsley
¼ teaspoon Tabasco sauce

6 SERVINGS

Prepare meat with tenderizer as directed on package. Combine ingredients in a shallow bowl or plastic bag. Add meat and marinate in refrigerator 6 to 12 hours or overnight. Place steak on rack 6 inches above hot coals. Grill 12 to 15 minutes, basting occasionally. Turn, continue basting and grill 10 to 15 minutes, basting occasionally. Turn, continue basting, and grill 10 to 15 minutes longer for medium done steak.

Tip: Grill 10 minutes per side for rare; 20 to 25 minutes per side for well done.

STEAK AND MUSHROOM KABOBS

½ cup dry red wine
½ cup cooking oil
1 clove garlic or ⅛ teaspoon garlic powder or instant minced garlic
½ teaspoon leaf marjoram, rosemary, basil or oregano
1 teaspoon salt
2 tablespoons catsup
1 tablespoon vinegar
1 teaspoon Worcestershire sauce
1 teaspoon MSG (mono-sodium glutamate), if desired
2 to 2½ lbs. family or sirloin steak, cut into 2-inch pieces
2 cups (16 oz. or 1 pt.) large fresh mushrooms or canned mushroom caps

6 SERVINGS

In plastic bag or mixing bowl, combine all ingredients except steak and mushrooms. Add steak and mushrooms. Turn or stir to coat with marinade. Close tightly. Let stand at room temperature for 2 hours or in refrigerator overnight. Drain and set aside. Thread meat and mushrooms on skewers. Broil 3 to 4 inches from heat, or grill over hot coals, turning occasionally until of desired degree of doneness.

KIND OF MEAT TO BARBECUE

		Temperature of Coals
Beef: Hamburgers	Make chunky for outdoor grilling.	Med.-Hot
Steaks	Tender cuts — sirloin, T-bone, porterhouse, club, rib. Less tender cuts — round or chuck. Use a meat tenderizer on these less tender cuts before grilling them. Tenderizers and marinades help make them more delectable.	Med.-Hot
Roasts	Rolled roasts are convenient for rotissing, but roasts with bones can also be used if the weight is balanced equally on the rod. Rib, high quality rump roasts, or less tender roasts that have been pre-tenderized can be cooked slowly over coals on a rotisserie. For less tender roasts that have not been pretenderized, marinate 12 hours or overnight before cooking on rotisserie.	Slow-Med. (rotisserie)
Pork: Pork chops	Buy at least 1-inch thick to cook over grill. Precook or be sure they are thoroughly cooked by cutting a slit in meat next to bone — no pink color should remain when done.	Slow
Spareribs	Precook in a large saucepan, covered with hot water and simmered over low heat for 45 min.; drain; marinate in barbecue sauces or brush with sauce during grilling and grill until tender and heated through, about 30 minutes. These can also be cooked on the rotisserie. Balance the weight by threading like an accordion.	Med.
Ham slices	Whether these are from a half fully-cooked ham or canned ham, cut them thick for grilling. Brush with sauce during grilling to give flavor and keep moist.	Slow-Med.
Fresh pork roasts	Cook these on the rotisserie — insert meat thermometer into center of leg; roast until 170° F.	Slow
Boned hams or large canned hams	Boned and rolled roasts are the most convenient, although others can be used if the weight is equally balanced. Rotisserie these cuts. The meat thermometer should read 160° F. when they are done.	Slow
Lamb: Leg or shoulder roasts	Cube these for kabobs to be grilled or, cook them whole, boneless, tied or netted on the rotisserie.	Med.-Hot
Chops, steaks, patties	Great for grilling! Brush with a marinade for special flavors.	Med.-Hot
Veal: Chops, steaks, cubes	For a marvelous rich flavor and moistness, marinate several hours in a zesty sauce or marinade before grilling. Baste often to keep moist.	Med.-Hot
Wieners and pre-cooked sausages	Need only heating through since they're ready to eat when purchased. To prevent curling, score. Try any kind of barbecue sauce.	Hot
Uncooked sausages	Cook thoroughly on grill.	Hot

To cook meats on the rotisserie, follow the instructions in your instruction manual:

- Center meat on spit so that weight is balanced equally.
- Thread ribs on spit in accordion fashion.
- When threading a cut of meat containing bone that runs the length of the meat, follow the bone, if possible.

- Meats over 12 lbs. generally do not cook well by rotisserie
- To avoid overbrowning when using a barbecue sauce, baste food only during the last 30 minutes.

GUIDE TO MEAT COOKING OUTDOORS

Type of Cooking		Examples
Grill (or broil)	Use foods that can be cooked quickly.	Steaks, chops, sausages, small fish, ribs (precooked).
Skewer	Almost any foods that can be skewered and will not fall off can be used for this type of outdoor cooking. Tougher cuts of meat can also be used if they are marinated to tenderize.	Beef, lamb, pork, veal, fish, chicken, sausages, ham, bacon, sweetbreads, shrimp, oysters, scallops. Vegetables such as zucchini cubes, cherry tomatoes, onion wedges, chives, green pepper chunks, sprouts. Fruits such as apple wedges, quartered pears, pineapple chunks, cantaloupe chunks.
Rotisserie (spit roasting)	Larger pieces of meat and poultry are ideal because of their self basting quality. A wire basket which can be mounted on the rotisserie rod can hold meat that might tend to fall off of rod.	Rolled and other large beef roasts, large steaks, large whole fish, lamb (leg, loin, rolled shoulder), pork (loin, shoulder, fresh ham, spareribs, suckling pig), poultry (chicken, cornish hens, squab, turkey), veal (leg, loin, rolled shoulder).
Smoke roasting	This is not the same as smoking (a curing process for ham). Smoke roasting is done by cooking in a covered barbecue for about the same time it takes to cook in oven. The end result is a definite smoked flavor.	Roasts, poultry (chicken, turkey), foods similar to those for rotisserie.

135

Grilled Steak

Meat in your meals

The meats or main dishes which you serve play an important role in your meal planning. Whether you approach meal planning on a weekly or a daily basis, the main thing to keep in mind is the overall balance of foods.

What you eat is reflected in your general health—your resistance to colds and other minor infections, the energy you have, and your outlook on life. A good fortification of vitamins C and A can set up a strong barrier against the various germs and illnesses to which children and adults are constantly exposed. The nutrients which you build into their meals can provide them with the resistance they need in order to stay healthy.

A careless pattern of eating can contribute to many minor ailments. Acne, tooth decay, chipped fingernails, dulled hair, and irregularity are some of the annoyances which can be influenced by your diet. Although we have enough to eat today, malnutrition from not eating the right kinds of foods is still a very serious problem. So, good health should be one of the most important considerations in your choice of food.

The essential nutrients, vitamins and minerals which are needed for good health are found in many types of food. Some of these nutrients are found more abundantly in certain foods than in others. Nutrition experts have provided a guideline for a balanced eating pattern in the basic four food groups. The foods have been categorized into four groups according to the proportions of each of the nutrients which they contain. By including a certain number of servings every day from each of these groups, you can be quite sure that your body is getting enough nourishment to keep it functioning properly.

A balanced pattern of eating can keep you feeling well and enjoying life! Using these groups as an overall daily guide, compare the foods that you usually include in your eating patterns with the number of servings that are recommended.

Meat, Poultry and Eggs: Meat, poultry, eggs, fish, nuts, dried beans and peas are included in this category. These foods supply the majority of the protein in the diet, as well as very good quantities of iron, minerals and B-vitamins. Infants, as well as adults, need foods from this group to maintain health. **Plan to have at least 2 servings a day from foods of this group.** For adults and adolescents, three ounces of cooked, boneless meat, fish or poultry is an average serving. Small children can get the food value they need from smaller servings. One egg, 2 tablespoons peanut butter or ½ cup cooked dried beans or peas are about equal in protein to 1 ounce of lean meat.

Milk and Dairy Products: Foods in this group are good suppliers of vitamins A and D, calcium and riboflavin and many contain good amounts of protein. Cheese, ice cream, and cottage cheese are some of the forms in which dairy products appear. Foods in this group can also be added to other dishes for variety. **Children need at least three or four glasses of milk a day; teen-agers, four or more; and adults, two.** The following quantities are about equal in calcium content to an 8 oz. serving of skim milk: 1⅓ cups cottage cheese, 1½-inch cube Cheddar cheese, and 2 cups ice cream.

Fruits and Vegetables: Four servings per day of foods in this group are recommended. One serving should be a good source of vitamin A (dark green or deep yellow vegetable), and one should be a good source of vitamin C (citrus, tomato, etc.) Other fruits and vegetables can be used to round out the day's menus; a serving is usually ½ cup. Since some of the vitamins in the foods of this group are dissolved in water or destroyed by heat, use the minimum amount of water and a short period of time to cook these foods. Foods in this group are good sources of vitamins C and A and some B-vitamins. In addition to vitamins, they also contain minerals, and some contribute roughage for healthy intestinal operation.

Breads and Cereals: Foods in this group provide iron, protein, thiamine, riboflavin, niacin and food energy. The foods included in this group are enriched, whole grain or restored breads and cereals, baked foods which are made with enriched or whole grain flour, enriched macaroni, spaghetti, and noodles. When bran and germ are removed in the processing of grains and cereals, food value is lost and these nutrients must be replaced. The food industry is required by law to "enrich" and "fortify" these products. If the cereal, bread or flour you buy is labeled "enriched", you can assume that the three B-vitamins and iron have been added. **Four servings of breads and cereals per day are recommended for good nutrition.**

Other foods not included in these four food groups can also be a part of your menus. Fats, oils, sugars and their products, as well as non-nutritive beverages (coffee, tea, pop, etc.) can be used to give interest. The nutritive value in most of these other foods is not high—although the calories in some of them are—so they should not be used instead of foods in the food groups. Include them only as extras.

The whole family, except for infants and those on medically prescribed diets, can usually eat the same basic meals. The amount of the various foods which different family members eat should vary according to the size and build of the person, his activity, and his stage of development.

Toddlers (1 to 3 years) need large amounts of protein-rich foods (meats, milk, etc.) because they are undergoing a very rapid rate of growth. The iron and B-vitamins found in these foods are essential to their growth and good health. Some of the frequently popular meats for this age group are ground or chopped meats (because of the ease in handling and chewing), bacon, and specially packaged canned meats.

Preschoolers (3 to 5 years) should have a serving from the meat group included in every meal, although the serving will, of course, be a smaller one than for other family members. Regular meats from the family table that have been conveniently cut for easy handling are well-appreciated at this age.

School children are still experiencing growth; adolescents are growing at a faster rate than at any other time in their lives except infancy. So, body-building minerals, vitamins and proteins are *extremely* important! Foods from the meat group should not only be included at meal times, but in snacks as well, where possible.

Adults usually become less active with age, and consequently need fewer calories. However, their needs for protein and other essential nutrients remain the same. When it becomes necessary to curtail calories because of weight problems, these excess calories should be removed from the non-essential foods, instead of from those in the basic food groups.

Pregnant or nursing women have greater needs for all of the nutrients. So, generous servings of protein-rich foods are essential to the health of the mother, as well as the baby-to-be. During these times, a minimum of two liberal servings of foods from the meat group should be included in the diet every day.

Balance is the key—sensibly consuming a variety of foods in reasonable quantities can keep you trim and fit and also give you the vitality to enjoy life to its fullest. What's more, it can add healthy years to your lives. What better gift could you give your family!

A balanced diet is important for good health, and food plays a unique and essential role in providing the nutrients needed for maintaining proper body functioning.

Your body is made up of cells which are chemical in nature. They depend on air, water and food to supply the chemicals they need in order to stay alive and to function properly. The foods which will provide your body with these important ingredients are ones that you're probably already familiar with. They contain the essential nutrients—proteins, vitamins and minerals, and the energy yielding fats and carbohydrates. These nutrients are composed of chemicals and usually come from plants and animals. Some of them can be stored in your body to be used later as they are needed; others can't be stored, so they must be a part of your *daily* food intake.

Digestion (breaking the complex molecules of food down into very simple ones which the cells can use) changes the foods which you eat into these nutrients. The nutrients are then carried by your blood to each of the cells, where they carry on the various functions which make your body run efficiently.

Carbohydrates: Carbohydrates are used in the body primarily as energy. However, some are also important in maintaining intestinal regularity. Carbohydrates are found abundantly in dried fruits, potatoes and other starchy vegetables, sugars, cereals and grains, fruits and vegetables.

Fats: Fats are the most concentrated form of energy, although energy is also found in carbohydrates and proteins. All excess energy that the body can't use is stored as fat. Some of this fat is necessary for insulation of the body against changes from hot to cold; other is used as protective cushioning for vital organs, such as the kidneys, heart and lungs. The rest of it is stored as excess fatty tissue until energy expenditure is high enough, or calorie intake is low enough, for it to be called into use. Fats are found in vegetable oils and animal fats; they add flavor to foods and make you feel full after eating.

Meat contains a marbling of fat between the tissues and around the muscles. Milk and milk products and nuts are also substantial contributors, although skim milk and other low fat dairy products have had most of this fat removed. Egg yolks, coconut and avocados are also foods of appreciable fat content.

Proteins: Protein must be present in every cell in the body and is used to build new tissue and to maintain and repair old tissue, as well as to regulate the balance of chemicals in the cells. Protein is also needed in the body to manufacture enzymes, hormones and antibodies which keep the body processes going and help guard against infections.

Proteins are made up of chains of amino acids. There are over 20 different amino acids which can form together into many different kinds of protein. Amino acids are the building blocks for protein just as bricks would be the building blocks for a fireplace. The body can synthesize some of these amino acids from chemicals that are derived from other foods. However, there are eight amino acids which the body is unable to manufacture and which are essential for the growth and maintenance of body tissue. In order for the body to be able to use these amino acids, they must all be present in the blood at the same time.

Some foods contain all eight of these essential amino acids; the proteins in these foods are called complete proteins. Foods that contain complete proteins are generally animal foods — meat, poultry, fish, eggs and milk. Several plant foods — dried beans and peas — also contain complete protein. These foods supply all the essential amino acids. Other foods, such as grain foods (flour, cereals, etc.) and many fruits and vegetables, contain only some of the essential amino acids. The body can use these as supplementary protein but cannot rely on them alone to provide adequate protein for proper body functioning. For this reason, it is important that some source of complete protein be served at every meal. If a meat, fish, poultry or egg dish is not served, include milk or cooked dried beans and peas along with the other foods.

Too little protein over an extended period of time can cause poor muscle tone and posture, slow recovery from surgery or illness, lowered resistence to disease, premature aging, anemia, stunted growth in children, and tissue degeneration.

Proteins, carbohydrates, and fats are the basic ingredients in all foods. Some foods have only one of them; butter, for example, consists mainly of fats. Others, such as meats, contain a combination of them. But in addition to these nutrients, foods also contain vitamins and minerals. Vitamins act as enzymes in digestion and in the use of nutrients by the cells. Minerals are necessary as a part of the chemical structure of the vitamins and of the cells which make up the body.

Vitamin A: Vitamin A is essential to the growth of children and to the general health of adults. It is especially important for healthy skin and vision. Vitamin A is also important inside your body to maintain the linings in your nose, mouth and body cavities. Liver tops the list of foods which contain vitamin A, but sweet potatoes, cantaloupe, dark green leafy vegetables, yellow-orange vegetables, apricots, tomatoes, egg yolks, and milk products are also good sources.

Vitamin C: Vitamin C cannot be stored by the body, so you need a good supply daily. It is essential for healthy tissue throughout your body, plays an important role in the growth and maintenance of teeth, bones, tissues and blood, and helps in healing wounds. Citrus fruits, strawberries, tomatoes, cauliflower, cantaloupe, cabbage, broccoli and other green vegetables, potatoes and green pepper are all good sources of vitamin C.

B-Vitamins: There are several B-vitamins. They are known by their chemical names: thiamine, riboflavin, and niacin are the principle ones. In general, meat is an excellent source of these vitamins and is generally the principal dietary supply.

Thiamine: Thiamine is used in the body to promote growth, good appetite, healthy nerves and good digestion. It is also essential to make the calories from carbohydrates and fats available for the body to use. Since thiamine can't be stored in quantity by the body, good sources of it should be included in meals daily. Good sources of thiamine are: lean pork, dried peas or beans, liver, vegetables, enriched and whole grain bread, cereals and grains, meats, fish, poultry, eggs and milk.

Riboflavin: Riboflavin also plays an important role in making the calories in fats, carbohydrates and proteins available for the body to use. It is necessary for good vision, healthy skin, and for growth. Riboflavin is not stored by the body in quantity, so foods that are rich in riboflavin should be included daily. Riboflavin is found abundantly in milk and milk products, liver, lean meat, salmon, eggs, enriched and whole grain bread, cereal and grains, and in green leafy vegetables.

Niacin: Niacin is important for healthy skin and nerves, and it has been shown to help in preventing nervousness, mental depression, and intestinal disorders. Dairy products, liver, fish, lean meats, poultry, enriched and whole grain bread, cereals, and flour, white potatoes, eggs, peanuts, and almonds are good sources of niacin.

Vitamin D: Vitamin D is needed by the body to make use of calcium and phosphorus in building strong teeth and bones. It is produced in the skin with the help of ultraviolet rays of the sun. It is also, in some places, added to milk.

The minerals which your body needs are a very necessary part of all cells and body fluid. In terms of getting enough to supply your body's needs, calcium and phosphorus, iron and iodine are the most important.

Calcium and Phosphorus: Calcium and phosphorus work together in the body and are important, not only for bones and teeth, but also for muscle contraction and nerve functioning. In addition, calcium is important in the clotting of blood. Milk and milk products, dried peas and beans, leafy green vegetables, salmon, crab and clams are very good sources of calcium. Phosphorus is found abundantly in dried beans, eggs, milk and other dairy products.

Iron: This mineral is necessary to form hemoglobin — the part of blood which transports oxygen throughout the body. Men and boys usually eat foods that provide enough iron for their bodies. Females, though, require larger amounts of iron because of periodic blood losses in menstruation. Too little iron in the blood shows up in a lowered capacity for work and in less vitality for daily activities. Liver, lean meats, dried beans, dried fruits, eggs, enriched and whole grain bread, flour and cereals, leafy green vegetables and shellfish contain iron in good quantities; however, supplementary iron in the form of pills is sometimes necessary.

Iodine: Iodine is required by the thyroid gland to produce a hormone which is essential in regulating the rate at which your body burns up energy. Seafoods and foods grown in soil near the seacoast are good sources of iodine in the diet; and iodized salt, which is widely available, is an excellent source.

Index